Game Planning & Play Calling in the Age of the RPO

RICH HARGITT

ISBN: 1729784690
ISBN-13: 978-1729784693

DEDICATION

This work is dedicated to my wonderful wife, Lisa and our beautiful sons Griffin and Graham. Thanks to my wife for all the endless support in coaching and to my sons for showing me what is really important in this life. Finally, this work is dedicated above all to God who gives me the ability to live each day with strength and honor.

CONTENTS

FOREWORD

As a football coach who has always known what he has wanted to do since he was on the sidelines with his Dad, it's amazing how fast 17 years has gone by. Growing up in Las Vegas, NV being part of a very run heavy era in the 90's when I got into the coaching profession I was always intrigued by being able to spread the ball around the field to as many players as possible. So, when I took over as the Head Coach at Coronado H.S. in 2017, I knew I had to bring with me a fun and fast style of play to spark the interest back into our program. With only 4 wins in the program the previous 2 years I knew coming in I would have to generate excitement from the MS level through the high school. Year one, we found decent success with a senior heavy roster with solid talent and went 4-6, but I felt I was missing something for our athletes to really be explosive.

Going into the offseason for season #2, I knew I had to simplify things but give the young athletes we had coming up a chance to make plays on the perimeter. I stumbled upon S2A as I was looking some different coaching sites and saw some things that Rich had been doing so I did a little research. I had always been skeptical about "systems" in the past, as it made me feel inadequate as a play caller. As I decided to reach out to Rich about S2A, I explained what I was looking for and he made sure to explain what and how he felt S2A could help our program out offensively.

After our conversation, I decided that this would be a great fit for Coronado football and I began to dive right into things. I first installed it with a 6th grade group in the spring, with my sons' team and they were able to grasp the concepts and did pretty well for first time players. Coming into the 2018 season I knew we were going to be inexperienced and have some young players on the field. I was pleased with how easy it was to install the S2A system and enjoyed how simple it was to communicate things to the players to be able to run it. We finished this season 4-6 and that may not seem like much, but I saw the progression of our QB's and skill players as the season progressed and how confident they were in what we ran, and they never felt out of a game. Our school and community really felt the buzz and backed us this season by coming out to support us more than our first year. It's an excited brand of football and they enjoy watching our team make plays.

Being part of Coach Hargitt's S2A system has been a true blessing for me as a coach in so many ways. The system is much more than just here is what we do, now go do it. This is a fraternity of coaches who run the S2A and we bounce many ideas off each other. I have personally grown a ton from this system and will continue to do so. Being part of the S2A is like having a whole other coaching staff on your team. The amount of time and energy that S2A gives its members is second to none and I am truly thankful to be a part of it.

Monte Gutowski
Head Football Coach
Coronado H.S. (Colorado Springs, CO)

1
THE DIFFERENCE BETWEEN GAME PLANNING AND PLAY CALLING

The terms game planning and play calling are used almost interchangeably in the world of football these days. The truth, however, is that these two concepts, while operationally similar, are quite distinct entities. The game of football has long been called half art and half science and this work will certainly share and expound upon that discussion but to build a quality offense in the modern era it is essentially necessary to be able to game plan (science) and play call (art) at an extremely high level in order to be an effective coach.

First, let us define these two ideas separately so that we might discern the actual difference between them. The science of game planning is fundamentally an idea that begins long before the lights flicker to life on a Friday night in some sleepy town or metropolis across the vast landscape of America. To provide a simple analogy let's think of a cake and the process of baking it. The game plan then principally serves as the batter and the ingredients all set out separately. A coach must determine what the defense looks like, what formations he will attempt to show or save, the general use of motion vs tempo, the run to pass distribution, and whether he intends to shorten the game with a series of run plays or elongate with an aerial free for all. These decisions are much like taking the ingredients of the bake and laying them all out on the counter and determining the flavor, size, and texture of one's favorite baked good. These ingredients will certainly affect the taste of the cake much like the game plan that the coach produces will affect the style of the game.

A game plan could also be thought of as the general strategies that will be employed in the game from the pace, to the aggressiveness, to the down and distance philosophies and whether the coach plans to take aggressive stances on fourth down. All these higher order thinking skills must be applied to the plan on Saturday or Sunday the week before the game will even be played. These ideas are thrown out in a montage of sometimes disorganized thoughts where they are refined and synthesized by a staff ranging from one person to maybe a half dozen or more. This plan will be altered, and strategies will be discussed, refined, and perhaps radically altered. The plan is fundamentally a blueprint that will be utilized by this coaching staff to score and agreed upon mythical number of points that should win the game the following Friday.

The art of play calling then is a completely different skill set and a different piece of framework for the modern offense. If we indulge the cake metaphor but a bit longer the play calling aspect of modern offenses is how long to bake the ingredients to determine moisture and then how to frost and decorate the cake to make it both aesthetically pleasing as well as satisfying to the pallet. In short, the art of play calling is just that, it is an art. Like all great works of art, they are not confined to the standard of anyone's critique but that of the artist. Most great play callers perform this art with assistance and with guidance, but they fundamentally decide what plays should be called based upon the taste of the game at that moment.

The play calling that occurs each Friday night is unique because each individual play caller attempts to make his work of art unique and more appealing that the person across the sideline from him. This flair for art makes its manifestation in the unique twist or seemingly random play call that might divert from the script because of an "intuition" on the part of the play caller.

There is the obvious statement that there is not good play calling without great game planning and it is also true that poor play calling can wreck a good game plan. These two ideas are, from the naked eye intertwined with one another, but they are still fundamentally different ideas that must be built with a different set of tools. There would, it seems, need to be a real-life example. Suppose that an offense had chosen the stance that they would not be aggressive at midfield because the goal of the game was to get first downs and maintain possession of the football, this is part of a sound and well thought out game plan.

Now let's suppose the play caller has the ball at the 50-yard line early in the game and calls Jet Sweep to the field only the defense calls a timeout once the motion starts and the play never happens. The play caller sees the defense rotate to man coverage and leave the backside receiver one on one with no safety help, he then calls the same motion but tags a vertical route to the single side receiver and strikes the defense for a massive 50-yard touchdown early in the game. Let's look at this situation in depth because it is a true situation the author dealt with this past fall.

The decision of the game plan to play for first downs when between the 20-yard lines was a sound strategy and was working quite well up until the defense called the timeout. The play caller then used artistic flair, nuisance, experience, intuition, whatever term you wish to apply that his gut told him that the man coverage he just saw on the backside of the formation could be exploited. To put it another way, the bakers had made a fine cake, but the icing needed a bit of panache. Therefore, the play caller transitioned from the world of strategic game planner into the world of Friday night play caller and made a choice that positively affected the outcome of the game. It is worth a note; this decision was deemed sound no matter what the result and no matter that it slightly altered the game plan because the strategy was good, but the tactics needed a small tweak.

Hopefully the idea that game planning is the major strategy of the game and the play calling is the tactics of how to execute that plan has shown through in this first chapter. As this work moves further along it will attempt to explain how both ideas intermix in what occurs on a Friday night. The game plan is an overarching strategy, but the goal of the game is to score points and win games. Therefore, the play calling sometimes must morph in order to make the results fit the model. It is worth pointing out that sometimes great play calling is to stick very close to the game plan as it was designed on Sunday and sometimes it is to jump off that status quo and work independently. That is why all great offensive coordinators are great game planners and great play callers because they can bake a great cake, but they also know how to decorate to make your mouth water.

2
BUILDING A GAME PLAN

There are principally four main considerations we make in the S2A System when we build a game plan and they focus around the formations, motions, personnel, and tempo that we will utilize in that game. Each of these items is instrumental in forming the plan and must be analyzed for how and when they will be utilized that week.

Formations

There is an old football saying that it is much easier to add a formation than add a play. This is never truer than in the modern game of football where there is a continuous trend toward playing the game faster on the offensive side of the ball and asking athletes to retain less information.

Philosophically, we believe that the game of football cannot be re-invented, but it can be recycled and re-packaged. In other words, as a base spread offense with heavy emphasis on RPOs we are just a modern-day evolution of the triple option style of football. We want to place the defense in conflict as much as we can to read defenders and make them play assignment-based football in order to prevent the defense's aggression and athleticism from being a contributing factor in the game.

Formational variations are a critical part of that equation because we feel if we can "change the picture" for the defense then we can make alignment very difficult for them. One of the greatest problems that modern defenses have is to get their personnel lined up and play the multitude of coverages, fronts and stunts that they have worked on throughout that week of practice.

Let's first start with a discussion of the basis of our formational philosophy.

At S2A we feel that all the plays that we utilize in each game plan must be able to be executed from a 2x2, 3x1, 3x2, and sniffer tight end set each week. We will certainly add other formational variations such as split backs, double tight end sets, and other unconventional and unbalanced formations in order to prevent the defense from grasping the structure of the offense. However, it is most important that all the plays in the game plan can be executed from those original base four formations. When those four formations are all involved in the game plan then the defense is forced to defend everything that an offense can throw at them. It is worth noting however, that there will be all sorts of new formational twists thrown at the defense in the first quarter of the game specifically to keep them from processing and getting too accustomed to those original base formations.

It is a philosophical belief that the whole offense can be run through those four base formations equally but that more information is better to keep the defense from settling in and understanding and focusing too much on those sets. We have opened games and used everything from a flexbone formation, to the I formation, to unbalanced and over sets in order to make each defensive coordinator process new looks. We do not add new plays from these formations but instead run our basic plays and RPO concepts. When we add three to four formational variances per week and progress say three games into the season, an opposing defensive staff may have as many as twelve new "looks" to process and prepare for instead of our basic four formations.

Motions

The use of motion has become quite an intriguing proposition for offensive coaches over the past few seasons. Some coaches believe that motion should be utilized almost every play while others feel it is an anomaly that simply takes too long to invest time into. At S2A, we feel that motioning players is an investment vs reward structure that must be analyzed every week versus every individual opponent. In short, if the use of motion benefits us as an offense then we will introduce it and utilize it during a given week. If we feel the use of motion does not confuse or distract from the defenses' assignments nor gives us a better picture of their intentions, then we will not utilize it that week. So, let us turn our attention to the types of motion we use.

The motions that we most utilize in S2A are Long, Short, Orbit, Bounce, Jet, and Fly. Long Motion is simply a receiver traveling across the formation and crossing the football to change the numbers for the defense. A simple example would be a 2x2 structure motioning into a 3x1 structure. This is down to determine if the defense intends to bump their coverage and or distort their box in order to combat the new formation. If the defense alters their alignment into a disadvantageous position or allows themselves to be outnumbered, then we are likely to use this motion but if no advantage is gained, we will not press the issue.

The close cousin to Long Motion is Short Motion. This is where a slot receiver will simply take a few steps as if he is in Long Motion before the ball is snapped. This motion is almost always used to simply identify man coverage. Once again, if the defense does not play any man coverage then we will simply not use this type of motion in that game plan.

Our third motion is known as Orbit Motion and is almost exclusively used by our H receiver to motion from a 2x2 or 3x1 alignment into a pitch relationship in the backfield with the quarterback. This can be down to change into a balanced or unbalanced receiver look for the RPO game or for the use of a triple option component for the offense.

Its close cousin is Bounce Motion where the H receiver is lined up in split back looks and quickly leaves the backfield. This is done to again take the defense from a balanced receiver look to one that is unbalanced or overloaded into a 3x1 structure. This is used to determine how defense will relate to two backs in the backfield and then attack them accordingly. Both motions are also very useful against man coverage teams to attempt to get small and quick H receivers onto slower linebackers.

Jet Motion is designed to simulate the Jet Sweep action of a slot receiver coming across the quarterback's path before disappearing to the flat. This motion is designed to allow the offense to trade a receiver across the formation while distorting the defense and their angles inside their structural format.

The final main motion that we utilize is Fly Motion. This is a motion from a 2x2 or 3x1 set into a 3x2 set with the running back leaving the backfield and resetting himself, unlike orbit or bounce, to create a pre-snap 3x2 structure to test the defense's answers to 3x2 formations very quickly before the snap.

All the motions mentioned above are simple to teach and very easy for the offensive play caller to signal in and identify defensive reactions to. That is the key for us to use a motion is to identify a reaction we want to analyze by the defense and then attack it accordingly. If we already know how a defense will align, then we oftentimes just line up in the formation and get a clear picture for the quarterback to process. A final consideration for the offensive play caller to consider is will the motion cause the defense to distort and confuse the quarterback's vision of the defense and his understanding of the defense's structure. All these considerations must be weighed and analyzed before introducing motion of the game plan. We have played games where we motioned a great deal and other games, we have used it almost none of the game. This determination should be made with careful and processed determinations of the effect on the defense and the effect on one's own quarterback.

Personnel

Personnel groups are another major consideration in the offensive game plan. Some coaches feel that changing these throughout the game is harder on a defense and some coaches feel that maintaining the personnel on the field is a better answer. We at S2A agree with both ideas and so we have constructed what we feel is a middle path on the idea of personnel. We train our X and Z receivers to be wide receivers and we train or Y receiver to play receiver, tight end, fullback, and sniffer.

The S2A H receiver is trained to play receiver, running back, and wingback while our running back is cross trained to play running back and receiver. This investment of time is a great advantage when it comes to coaching at a school with low numbers, but it is also a great was to get all your players to really grasp the game of football better. When players cross train they understand each other's' roles and are therefore more knowledgeable, like a quarterback, about the whole game plan. However, the main reason we do this is that it allows us to change personnel structure, which is very hard on a defense, but to do so without subbing new players in and therefore prevents the defense from subbing in new players for reasons of conditioning or assignment type.

A great way to think about personnel in the S2A System is that it is like a chameleon. If we want to play with a tight end our Y receiver does that and forces the defense to cover a tight end, but the defense is stuck on the field and can't sub a player in that specializes in attacking or jamming tight ends, instead the defense is forced to stay with the personnel on the field.

If the offense wants to play with five wide receivers the running back fills that whole and does not allow the defense to sub into a nickel or dime situation. This inability to flex their positions and personnel puts the defense at a distinct disadvantage while allowing us to morph ourselves into a personnel group that has the most adverse effect on the defense. We can go fast or slow (tempo to be discussed below) but we are a working chameleon that adapts itself to our environment and makes the defense adjust to us instead of us adjusting to them.

We strive to start and finish a drive with the same players who are like Swiss Army knives that can be multiple attack tools while the defense is forced to guess what type of athletes to put on the field while the offense morphs and adjusts into structures that cause the most assignment and personnel conflicts for the defense that we can create on a given possession.

Tempo

Tempo is the last major consideration to be discussed in this chapter about building a game plan. There is a major misconception that tempo teams must always play fast and go at a breakneck speed in order to be effective. While the need to go fast is often valuable and very often required to win sometimes it is working against the benefits of the offensive game plan.

A major consideration about tempo use in a game plan should be centered on two main factors. The first factor is whether the defense is confused using tempo. There are many defensive teams that will simply play base defense and make almost no major adjustments to tempo and have base checks that keep them aligned correctly versus the offense's changing formations while in a tempo situation.

These types of defenses are not really harmed by fast tempo and therefore it is not necessarily relevant to go faster against them. However, if the defense misaligns and makes major structural mistakes versus a faster tempo then it might be necessary to speed the game up and attempt to make them incorrect. If the defense can handle fast, then slow down and if they prefer slow then speed up. This should be a major emphasis in scouting and preparing for a given opponent each week in the game plan.

A second major consideration for the offensive play caller is whether the opponent can take advantage of a fast paced and long game. A classic example is a wing-t style team that huddles before the play is not likely to take advantage of a fast-paced game and extend the game to three or more hours and fatigue your defense if you are playing fast. If, however, you are playing another spread tempo style team and they can score fifty points in a three hour or longer game then this must be a second contributing factor in the use of fast tempos. An analysis of what your team's defense can handle must play into this consideration. If the offensive play caller thinks they can with a 57-56 shootout that takes over three hours to play, then perhaps it is a great time to ramp up the tempo and go fast.

If, however, the play caller's defense needs help then perhaps a two-and-a-half-hour game is better suited, and a slowed down tempo is better so that you might win a game 24-17. Essentially, an offensive play caller must decide whether the tempo of the game should be used to extend the time of the game and make it longer with more possessions or shorter with fewer possessions. This should not be accomplished in a vacuum but should be a part of a consensus among the two coordinators as well as the head coach about the overall strategic plan of attack for that week. I have won games where I reduced the number of possessions as well as increasing them for strategic reasons based upon my analysis of both my and the oppositions capabilities on both side of the ball. This sort of analysis is essential for tempo, whether slow or fast, to be utilized correctly and to its greatest benefit in winning a football contest.

Conclusion

As we discussed above there are four main considerations, we make in the S2A System when we build a game plan and they focus around the formations, motions, personnel, and tempo. These four items must not operate inside a vacuum but be openly discussed and debated by a good staff each week in order to formulate the best game plan possible. The days are gone where an offensive play caller sits down and simply decides what to call and when to call it oblivious of the special teams and defensive considerations of the football program.

Instead, a holistic approach to building an offensive game plan must consider not only these four major considerations but also items such as weather, homecoming, injuries, and a whole host of other items that could fill journals of pages when considering their impact. It is essential that these considerations are weighed openly and honestly, and the game plan is formulated with the end goal of what is best for the whole program and not the passing whim or ego of any play caller in question.

3
THE TRINITY OF GAME PLANNING

There are three major considerations that go into the final phase of game planning for an S2A Offensive game plan. These three items are the last major consideration that should be made before a coach finishes the game plan and proceeds to play calling the night of the game. The trinity consists of matchups, leverage, and grass. This portion of game planning is different than what was discussed in the previous chapter in that all three of these items are a specific comparison and analysis of the defense that you will be playing.

These items principally concern how the defense has aligned and whether they have done so "correctly" or not. The items from Chapter 2 talked about what we as an offense might utilize and how we wished to do it. For instance, the use of formations is principally controlled by what type of athlete's my offense has each year and what those athletes are capable of accomplishing. This chapter will focus instead on three items that, while still concerning the type of athletes I have, will look a great deal more at the defense and their structure and makeup. The trinity of game planning includes an analysis of matchups, leverage, and grass.

Matchups

The first item to be analyzed in game planning is the number and type of matches advantages that the offense possesses. This essentially translates into which of our players can defeat which of their players in a one on one matchup. This matchup advantage can take place all over the field. It can be an X receiver that is tall taking a natural matchup advantage over a shorter corner. It could be a shifty H receiver taking advantage of a slower linebacker type player. The matchup advantage might be an aggressive offensive lineman that can push around a smaller and less strong defensive lineman. The point to the matchup conversation is that it is a naturally occurring offensive advantage that is already on the field simply by the type of players that you already have in your program.

The second consideration about matchups is that the offensive coach might have to manipulate these advantages to his team's benefit. Defenses are likely to recognize their natural weaknesses and attempt to cover them up. They may play their tallest and most rangy corner on your best tall receiver for instance. It is not acceptable to just leave this athlete at this position where he may or may not be able to influence the game. A coach might have to motion this receiver away and create a different matchup on a worse defender.

The offensive coach might be able to move this receiver to the slot at times and isolate him on a linebacker. The point is that it is up to the offensive coach to make these matchups happen. Some defenses will allow natural matchup advantages by the offense to go unchecked but oftentimes they will cover these weaknesses. When this occurs the offensive game planner must adjust and recreate advantageous matchup situations wherever and whenever possible.

This is an important and often overlooked skill for offensive game planning. Many coaches will say that they have no matchup advantages, the more likely truth is that he has simply not created them and manipulated the defenses into allow them. This can and must be done each week in the game plan and should be the first item of this trinity in game planning that should be addressed each week.

Leverage

The second item to discuss in the game planning conversation is the issue of Leverage. Leverage is defined as the way the way a defender plays head up, inside, or outside of an offensive player. This leverage is, once again, something that either occurs naturally or as a result of how the defender chooses or his assignment dictates him to line up. These alignments then cause the defense to be able to take away certain features of the offense's attack.

An example would be a slot receiver being covered to the inside by an outside linebacker. This inside leverage prevents the offense from easily executing any inside breaking route. However, the defense is out leveraged to the outside. This means that the offense has an outside advantage on any route concept that might break to the outside or the offense can down block this out leveraged defender and run outside of him. The game plan must consider the basic leverages that the defense utilizes and when and if these leverages change based upon down and distance tendencies. Some defenses will alter their leverage on short or long yardage while other defenses choose to keep these leverages standard and never alter them unless forced to do so by the offense.

As with all aspects of planning for an opponent, the offense can alter and take advantage of leverage assignments. For example, if the slot receiver has the defender out leveraged to the outside the offensive player knows this but so does the defender. The defender may play inside leverage and then jump yard on an outside stemming route. In this case it may need to be included in the game plan for the receiver to use routes that stem outside and force the defender to attack that voided area outside to open his hips and allow the receiver to win back to the inside.

All these sorts of leverages and their advantages and alterations need to be considered for that week's opponent by the offensive game planner. These items must be analyzed through film study and coaches should be trained to watch alterations inside the game on the night of the contest to make sure these leverage relationships match what was identified on film study.

Leverages are usually standard, but defenders do change, and defensive coordinators will make athletes change during the contest. It is our belief that once a defender starts altering his leverage the defense can quickly become unsound and attacked in a variety of new and exciting ways.

Grass

The third and final portion of game planning consideration when analyzing the defense is the use of Grass. The analysis of Matchups and Leverage are standard and easy to explain. The idea behind Grass is a more abstract concept. Defenses align in ways that allow Grass to be exposed and open to attack even when they align correctly. A great example is a 2x2 set into the boundary. The defense can cover the outside receiver soft over the top with the outside linebacker covering the slot receiver basically head up. This set would allow there to be a fair amount of Grass over the top of the outside receiver between him and the corner.

The offense could use the slot to block the corner and throw the ball to the outside receiver. The amount of Grass between the corner and the ball and the outside linebacker and the ball is too great for those athletes to close before the receiver can get a 5-yard gain in many cases. This is not because of a matchup and it is not because of a leverage issue but because the defense gave up a small area of Grass and the offense figured out how to take advantage of it.

The Grass can be found in a wide variety of places. Sometimes the grass is over the guards when the defense plays a 3-2 box with their defensive ends lined up too wide. In this case a 1 back power play into the box might be the best way to "Attack the Grass." The goal of the game planner is to identify where these areas of Grass are located and then how best to design a blocking scheme or route combination to take the greatest advantage of this scenario. Many times, a naked eye can spot the Matchup or Leverage advantage the offense has but it takes a trained and experienced eye to identify the Grass and how best to change the surface of the offense to make that Grass an advantage for the offense and a liability for the defense.

Conclusion

The idea of identifying Matchups, Leverage, and Grass is the basis for how a Surface to Air System style offense will determine how and where best to attack an opponent. The Matchup portion is the easiest to identify but sometimes the hardest to manage. A coach must decide where these matchups can be most directly advantageous to the game plan and then move players around the field like knights on a chessboard. This is a long and evolving, yet not too difficult, structural process.

The ideas of Leverage and Grass oftentimes work in concert with one another. If the offense can establish a consistent advantage in leverage somewhere than the coach can call plays that take advantage of this and repeatedly go back to that well and harm the structural integrity for the defense. If, however, Leverage is not given away by the defense they will oftentimes as least leave area of Grass that can be attacked. Even if the defense plays press man coverage, they leave large areas of Grass behind all the defenders all the way back to their own end zone.

These are not all knowing or comprehensive assessments of how to build a game plan for the game of football but what they are tried, tested, and true identifiers of how the author has analyzed defenses and attacked them for close to 20 years. These ideas provide a sound and stable platform for preparing to attack the defense. These ideas are also the basis for all the concepts and plays that will inhabit the following chapters of this book and they form the solid backbone of game plans to allow the play calling of the game to show through more reliably and successfully on Friday Nights.

4
PLAY CALLING: THE NIGHT OF

A simple answer to what game planning is versus play calling might be explained quite simply. In the Surface to Air System: game planning is what you do until game time on Friday Night and Play Calling is what you do starting at kick off. It should be stated that if the game planning portion of the offensive attack is lacking then it is essentially irrelevant how good of a play caller a coach is on game night. This is to say that there is no realistic way to call a good game on Friday Night if the work of game planning has not been adequately handled prior to the start of the kickoff. The preceding chapters have attempted to analyze and synthesize the process of game planning ahead of the kickoff whereas this chapter is designed to handle the more direct aspects of play calling after the kickoff.

Play calling on the night of a high school football game is a lot more than just going out and deciding which play to call. It is really a labor of love in which you must analyze not only the opponent but also yourself and determine whether that opponent does certain things well or does certain things poorly and then do the same self-evaluation for your own team. It is really in a very simple sense a lot more about finding out who you are then it is about finding out what your opponent is trying to do although both are critically important. It is necessary to go out and analyze where you are in terms of injuries, tempo, expectations and where you are at this point in your season and determine all those sorts of things before you call that first play on Friday night.

Play calling on the night of the game is a huge work of art and it takes years to craft it in just the right way. The first thing that must be done is a coach must decide what are going to be the openers for this game. What openers really mean is how does the coach intend to start out the game what sort of formations do you intend to use what sort of plays do you plan to come out and try to strike quickly and get on the board or you just trying to get first downs you really need to decide what type of opener you want to start the game with. After a coach has determine his openers it is next necessary to go through and decide what sort of philosophy you're going to have on first down, second down, third down and if necessary fourth down. There should also be a clear-cut understanding of what you're going to do if you are backed up in your own end zone, if you are in the middle of the field, as you approach the red zone, and finally what happens when you get into the red zone.

These sorts of situational play-calling strategies must be analyzed in the game plan of time but what a coach does in each of these situations is critically important. As we said earlier game planning is what you do in the days leading up to the football game but on Friday night these sorts of decisions must be made in a split second. There are many things that go into the game plan and there is always a great plan laid out by any well-prepared offensive coach however, as has been said many times, everyone has a great plan until the first time they get hit. Great play-calling is not an execution of the game plan great play-calling is really what happens after the first few mistakes are made and the first few parts of the game plan begin to unravel. Game-planning then is really what you do as an adjustment each time you call a play the game plan will almost never follow the script 100% start to finish. If game plans followed the script from start to finish without any deviation, then almost anybody could be a great play-caller but that's simply not the truth in most football games.

What must be done when the quarterback throws an interception or the running back trips and falls or the offensive line holds, and you suddenly find yourself in a 1st and 20 situation or your backed up at your own 2-yard line? The answer to that problem is play calling.

How do you adjust the game plan to reflect new play calls that help you manage situations as they arise? It is this sort of thinking on your feet that really involved the key art of play-calling and someone who cannot think on their feet quickly and cannot make these adjustments in split-second decisions is not quite prepared for the play-calling section of the game. Having said all of that, some people can learn to game plan from a manual. Not everyone can learn how to play call out of a book or out of a manual. Play-calling is really something that is done through hours of testing and trial and failure and is done each week until a person becomes good at it.

Play calling is also not something that can be passed down from one to the other and each coach having the same style. Play calling is an art that each coach must define for himself and must figure out how best to do inside his own framework and inside his own system.

The Surface to Air System features a large amount of information to help our members call plays more effectively. Included in these sections are openers, P&10, 1st and 10, 2nd and short, 2nd and medium, 2nd and Long, 3rd and short, 3rd and medium, 3rd and long, 4th Down, coming out, and all the different ways to attack defense is based upon field position including the red zone. All these different types of down-and-distance tendencies and what you should do in each category and how you should approach them philosophically is really then the nuts and bolts of what the rest of this book will be about.

This book is designed to be a case study from the 2016 and 2017 seasons on what I have done calling plays in each of these categories and what I feel works best in each specific section. This book will also include my basic philosophy for what a play caller should be attempting to achieve in each individual section. For instance, if the call that is coming up for a play-caller is 2nd and short there is not only a specific list of plays that have been proven over the last two seasons to be very effective but there is also an overall and general philosophy that should be maintained by the coach.

To put this more succinctly the goal of the surface-to-air offense on 2nd and short is basically to convert to first down. There will be four basic plays outlined in that chapter that will show the reader how in 2016 and in 2017 the surface-to-air system was successful in converting 2nd and short to a 1st and 10. While these plays are not the only nor comprehensive list of plays that could be utilized in this down and distance they are tried and true and proven plays that have worked over the past two seasons. The overall philosophy of converting on 2nd and short and why the author believes that a conversion is the best strategy on 2nd and short instead of for instance taking a shot and attempting to score a touchdown will also be outlined in each individual chapter of this book.

It then becomes a game of downs and distances and field-based tendencies that really drive home the basis of the surface-to-air system. Of course, the style of defense being faced the hash and or the boundary tendencies of that defense will always make a big and lasting contribution into how you should play call. However, it is the fundamental belief of the author that the down-and-distance should be the driving force of what the offensive play-caller is attempting to achieve. There should also be special consideration taken by the play caller into where the ball is currently located on the field.

Throughout the week I feel that play-calling is about understanding yourself and your own football players out on the field and what you were attempting to accomplish in that game. While the thoughts and ideas in this book serve as a general basis for play calling and they are not the only answer to a specific situation. There are certainly times when in 2nd and short that we might elect to take a shot at a touchdown instead of a conversion to 1st and 10. This may be caused by the way the defense has reacted toward a situation that I have addressed or a matchup that I may have noticed on the field at a time. This work is simply to serve as the blueprint and the scaffolding that we are currently utilizing. Each football coach must make play calling an integral part of his own personality.

Conclusion

This work will attempt to dive deep into the psyche of a play caller. This work will attempt to provide the basis for how a football coach could call a modern spread offense of this type of system that is based heavily on RPOs. This work should be considered both what it is and what it is not. This work is a basis for play calling but each individual coach should always be open to the idea of putting his own touches on play calling and allowing his own artistic flair to come through.

The two major emphasis that should be taken away from play-calling in this book is that down and distance is a heavy part of how play should be called, and the second major point is that the position on the field should be also a major contributing factor in what types of plays are called. As was said previously, all play callers will add their own individual artistic impression to their own style of play calling. This work is the manifestation of several years of work and research into how the art of play-calling really meets the science of game planning and how those two items move together in lockstep to produce a quality offensive system.

5
OPENERS

Openers are the way in which a play caller chooses to start a football game. The openers are meant to send a message to the defensive coordinator in how the play-caller is going to try to run this football game. In the surface-to-air system it is my preference to always use openers to send the message that this will be a very difficult game from an intellectual standpoint for the defense to attempt to play.

I want to convey two major messages with my openers; the first message I want to convey is that I will be very aggressive trying to score touchdowns, the second message I want to convey is that I will be using a great deal of formations, motions, and other types of changes in order to confuse the defense. The opener that I choose to utilize can change from week-to-week and often does. I do not think that the opener needs to be nor, should it be the same against every opponent every week. The openers are really the way in which the offensive play-caller should attempt to put his stamp on the game.

There are many times where my openers actually have very little to do with how I intend to call the game. Sometimes I will want to call a very aggressive game, so I will call very aggressive openers but at other times I will want to have a more conservative game plan where I rely on my defense in my kicking game and call a very aggressive set of openers.

Sometimes I'm going to play reckless go-for-broke style of offensive football and I may start out with very conservative openers. Each week's openers should be tailored to send the message non-verbally across the sideline that the offensive play-caller wants to convey to the defensive coordinator, his staff, and his players. I feel that openers are really the way to start out a conversation. I want to start out in a variety of different sets.

So often, my openers are a manifestation of my desire to move the defense around and dictate the style of play that I wish to play. Therefore, most of the time my openers will include formations that may not be traditional, motions that may not be normal, and generally plays that are designed to send some sort of specific message.

Examples of Game Openers

As was stated above, openers will often change from week to week. These plays should be designed to send a message to the defense each week. Also, as was stated previously, these examples that follow are all examples of openers that we have utilized in our record-breaking offensive years of 2016 and 2017.

The first such opener that I want to explain is the Unbalanced Jet Play (Diagram 5-1).

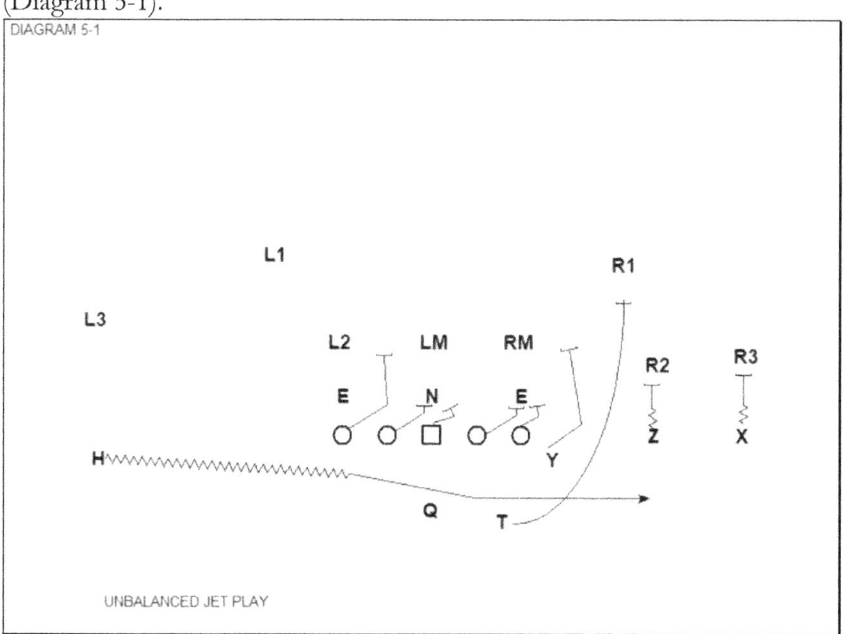

In this play we are bringing our X and Z receivers over into an unbalanced look and adding a sniffer set to the equation. These three athletes allow us to outnumber the defense with the exception of the hash safety or the R1 defender in our Surface to Air System nomenclature. This athlete is accounted for by allowing the tailback to be set to the unbalanced side and sending him to attack the R1. The H receiver will be brought in Jet Motion and shoveled the ball to execute the end around action against the defense. The offensive lineman will simply execute aggressive outside zone footwork.

The reason this play is a great play to use as an opener is because it involves several components that defenses will not like. This play involves using an unbalanced formation, a sniffer Titan set, a running back to the 3-receiver side, and Jet motion from the h receiver. All these components combined make it very difficult for the defense to process what is being done to them and it gives the offensive coordinator a great opportunity to look at the defense and see how they handle a variety of situations. These situations include: how does the defense processes unbalanced sets, how does the defense process a sniffer tight end set, and how does the defense handle motion. The offensive coordinator is then able to see how the defense will handle this variety of situations while also getting himself a big opening play and getting the ball into one of his playmaker's hands at the very beginning of the contest.

The next type of opener that has shown itself to be successful the last few years is a play that we in the Surface to Air System call Crazy (Diagram 5-2).

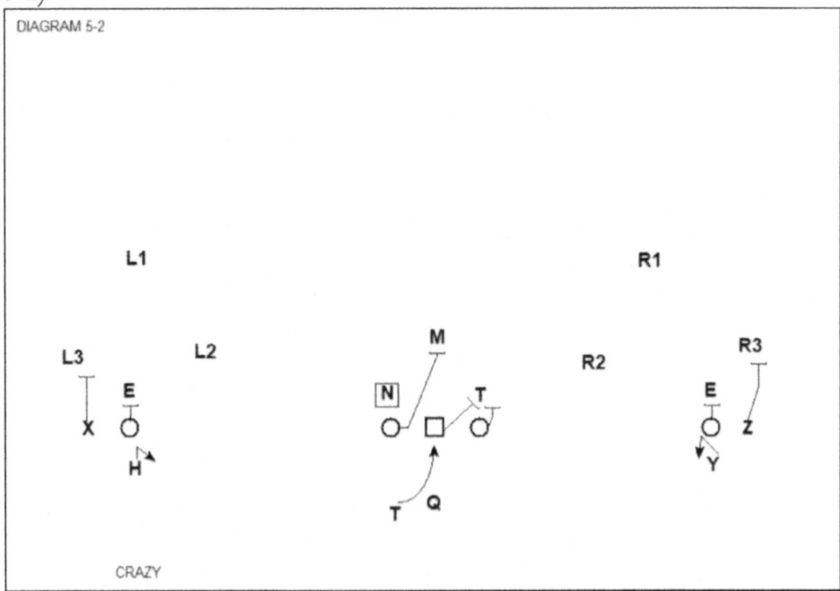

The crazy play has the advantage that the offensive tackles are split out wide and are with two receivers on the numbers to each side of the field. The center and guards remain in their normal alignment and therefore the quarterback is still able to run zone-read style football in the box.

A simple check by the quarterback is to look to the outside pods and determine whether he has a 3 on 2 advantage and can throw the ball to either pod located out on the numbers. If the quarterback is not able to execute the throw to one of those pods, then he can very simply read the remaining defenders in the box and play zone-read football. This is an excellent way to spread the defense out from sideline to sideline and determine how well the defense can run to the football. One of the major components of our system is analyzing whether the defense can identify formational variations and finding out whether they are able to run to the football and make tackles in wide open space.

This is a sort of formation and play that allows us to analyze both of those components simultaneously and make a couple great determinations about whether the defense is prepared to play our style of football effectively. This is also a great way to get the ball to playmakers in space and hopefully get a cheap 1st down to start the football game.

Defenses will oftentimes realize that we wish to get the ball out of the quarterback's hands early in the contest and get quick 1st downs. When the defense realizes this, they will oftentimes attempt to jump these quick passes and see if they can get an early turnover. It is therefore useful to utilize a Joker Play early in the contest to keep the defense on their toes (Diagram 5-3).

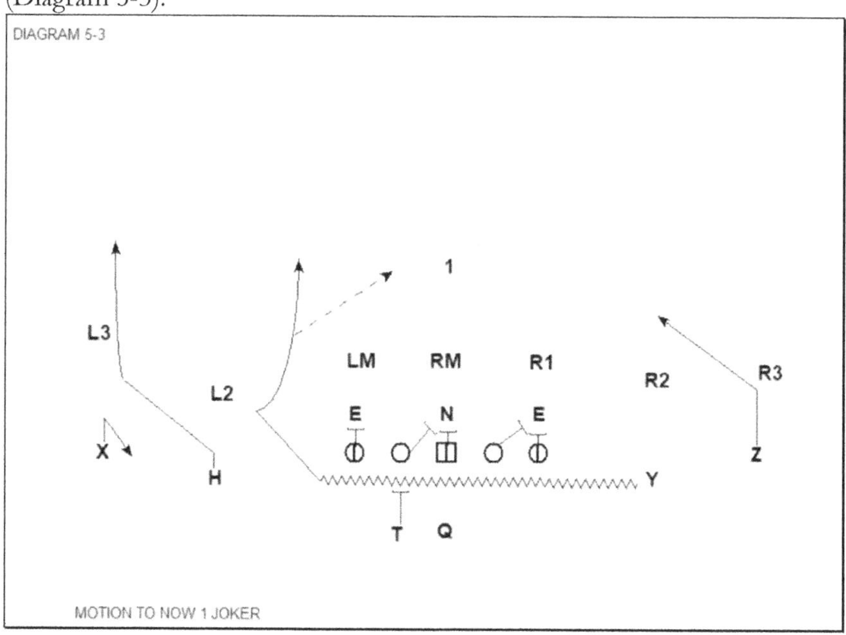

So, let's assume that the defense is going to be playing some sort of 1 high structure right here. the offense will come out in a standard 2x2 set and utilize motion into a 3 x 1 set. this serves to allow the offensive coordinator to determine how the defense intends to handle motion from a balanced to an unbalanced set. The offensive coordinator can elect to go ahead and throw now screens to the perimeter and take advantage of any numerical superiority that may be achieved in the flat. However, a great way to start the football game is to go ahead and throw in a now Joker play and take advantage of the defense's tendency to jump routes early in the game. If the play is successful, then it's very likely the offense will be up a touchdown after their first possession. If, however the defense sniffs out the Joker play, attacks it, and prevents it from being a score the offensive coordinator has still accomplished his main goal which is to send a message to the defense they should not jump quick routes in the flat.

This sort of play serves as a constraint against the defense and the defensive coordinator from jumping quick breaking routes. This sort of play included in your openers list will allow you to throw more high-percentage quick throws that enable your quarterback to have success throughout the game because you have backed the defense off and warned them early in the contest.

Sometimes it is necessary for the offensive coordinator to get into a heavy set and simply play some smash-mouth football with the defense at the start of the football game. It is a great idea, if the offensive coordinator feels like he has the Personnel to do so, to get into a heavy formation and hit the defense and be physical with them early in the contest to see what sort of defensive fronts and character that will create. A great way to do that is by bringing in two sniffers and running inside zone with a double split kick out by those two sniffers from a pistol set (Diagram 5-4).

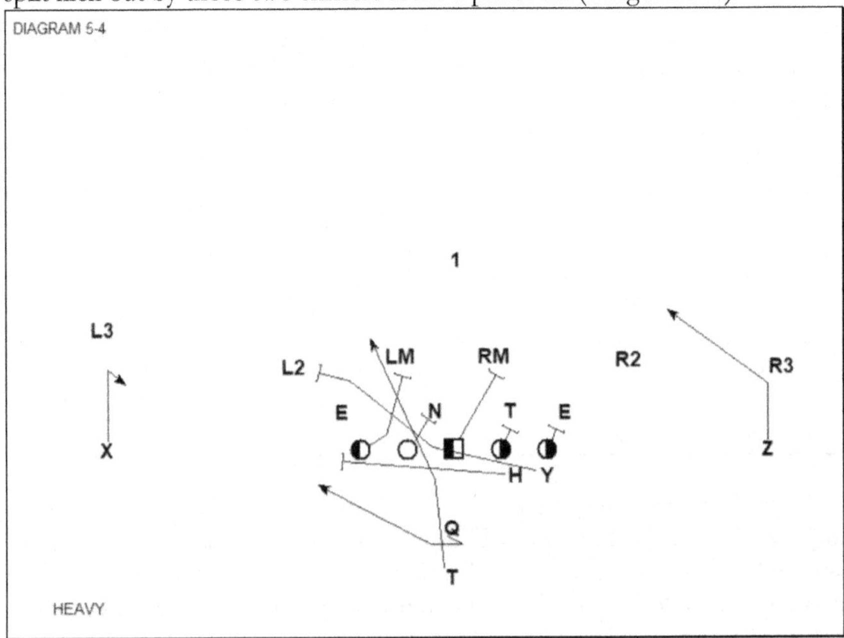

This formation and its personnel grouping might be hard to utilize later in the game as some of the personnel might be borrowed from the defense. It is best to use these heavy sets early in the game before those linebacker type of players off your defense have become fatigued from playing multiple quarters of defense. This is another way to send a message to the defensive coordinator that you intend to be physical and attempt to run the football as a standard part of the game plan.

Conclusion

It is an important part of calling plays to understand what openers are and why they are being utilized. Openers should be a way for the offensive coordinator to send a message not only to the defensive staff but also to his own sideline.

These plays are a way to demonstrate how and where and with what sort of physicality the offense of coordinator intends to call the game. It should also be said that openers should draw the eye of the defensive coordinator to what the offensive coordinator wants him to see. These plays for me are essentially a way for me to mess with the head of the defensive coordinator and show him things and established precedents for later in the game. I want to make the defensive coordinator worry about formations and motions and other sorts of twists and variations that may or may not be a part of the overall game plan.

I am also looking to establish tempo with many of these openers being one-word calls that we created for that week. Lastly, I am attempting to get cheap first downs and big chunks of offense yardage where I know I can flip the field at a bare minimum make sure that I can punt the football onto my opponent's end of the field or even get a cheap touchdown or field goal to start the contest. I have long felt that openers are a critical part of being an effective play-caller in a system like ours but unfortunately, they are one of the more underutilized and undervalued aspects of play-calling in the modern game of football. I feel that these plays should be emphasized and discussed and be a useful part of every offensive coordinator's repertoire when he goes into a game. These are also a fun and exciting "Strike Up the Band" sort of plays and send a message to both sidelines that you intend to come out and play fast and to play physical in each contest.

6
P & 10

P and 10 is the first set of downs on any sort of change of possession in the game of football. So, in other words if you get a fumble or interception or any sort of turnover and there is a dramatic change of downs it means the first possession you have after that. Sometimes in both college and in NFL football it's referred to as a sudden change of possession. What we are really analyzing here is what plays to call right after you have gotten the football back on any kind of change of possession.

It could be something as subtle and simple as your defense forcing a punt and your offense taking possession of the field. It could also mean a turnover. So therefore, P and 10 is the first possession of any offensive drive it need not be a possession that changes with a dramatic turn over but could just be a punt that you are receiving. The point is this is an undervalued and under realized portion of the game of football.

A coach might ask why this set of downs is so critical and why it is just not listed as a 1st and 10 set of downs. The reason why this set of downs is so critical is it will set the tone of what the play-caller is attempting to accomplish. A play caller may decide that these sorts of plays should be big and exciting, and he should "Go for Broke."

A play caller may also decide that these plays should be a simple quick game or easy play to move the chains. A play caller may also decide to be more conservative. There are a wide variety of things that have to do with the first set of downs after a change of possession. That list is long, and this chapter is not going to be an attempt to set up a comprehensive list. Instead this chapter will include an aggressive down field drop back pass, a quick game type of pass play, a play-action pass play call, and finally a simple RPO type pass play with a run attached. All these plays could be the right play to call in a P and 10 type of situation it is up to the individual offensive coordinator to decide which is best. So, this chapter will attempt to provide examples from both the 2016 and 2017 Seasons that meet all the above-mentioned criteria for a P and 10 style set of downs.

P and 10 Example Plays

The first example in this section of plays will be a "Go for Broke" and type of play. The best example of this sort of down the field drop back pass is the 4 Verticals Concept (Diagram 6-1). This play will feature Fade Routes by the outside receivers and Seam Read bender Routes by the slot receivers. The tailback will execute a check down route as part of his pass protection responsibilities.

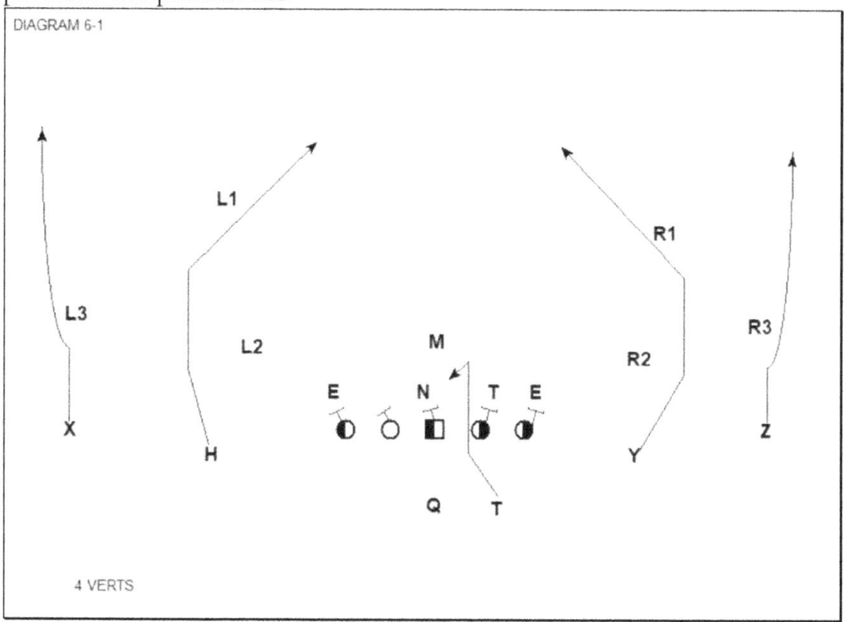

A coach might decide to use this sort of play because it will immediately test the back end of the defense's capabilities. One of the quickest ways to determine if a defense is sound is to run four receivers vertically and find out if the defense can cover all four and the corresponding grass around them. This is also a great way to send a message to the defense at the start of a new possession that you intend to be hyper aggressive. Because the tailback can run the check down route or be put into the flat on a wide variety of other routes the quarterback has a safe place to dump the football off to and make this a safe pass play if the defense were to be dropping too many defenders.

A second way that a coach might elect to start a new possession is with a quick pass play out of a 3x2 structure. This type of pass play forces the defense to spread themselves out across the entire field and play the formation honestly. If the defense chooses to bring pressure or sit back in a zone coverage, this tells the offensive play caller a great deal about the intentions of the defensive coordinator. This sort of information should be cataloged and remembered as it can be usefully utilized throughout the possession. An easy sort of pass play might be a Spot Concept paired with a Slant Option Concept (Diagram 6-2).

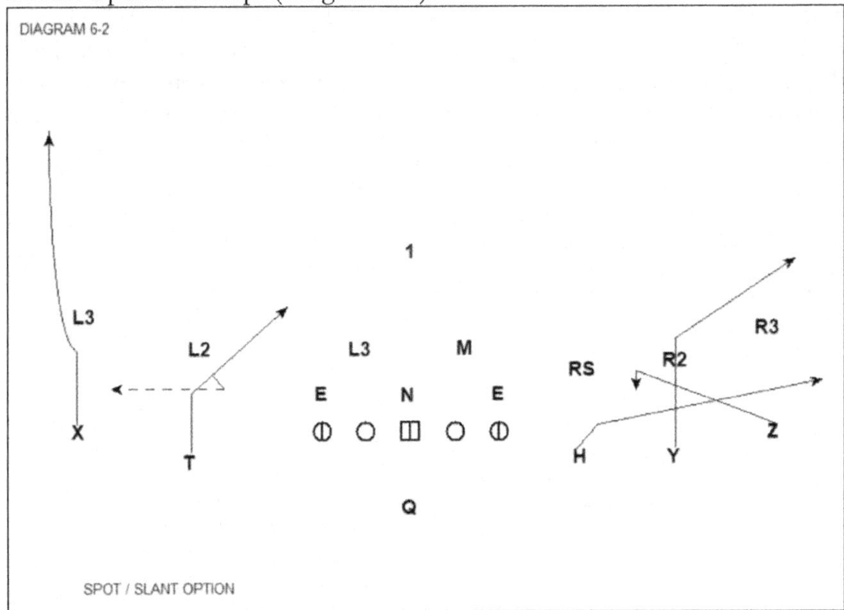

This sort of pass play is easy to execute and gives the quarterback a multiple coverage beating aspect to both flanks regardless of how the defense lines up. Both concepts can attack man or zone coverage. Again, the point of these plays in a P and 10 situations is to certainly get 1st downs but it is also to answer questions about how the defense will respond to certain formations and certain plays. This sort of pass call will immediately tell the offensive play caller how the defense will elect to attack his quick game options.

A third type of play that a play collar may wish to utilize in a P and 10 situations is a play-action pass or PAP call. This sort of play allows the play-caller to fake a commonly used Run play and then take a vertical shot behind the back of the defense. This allows the offensive coach to not only see how the defense is defending run plays but also see how disciplined defensive backs are in maintaining eye contact with receivers versus looking into the backfield. A great play to utilize then is the Double Post Concept off a Gap Scheme run such as the One Back Power Play (Diagram 6-3).

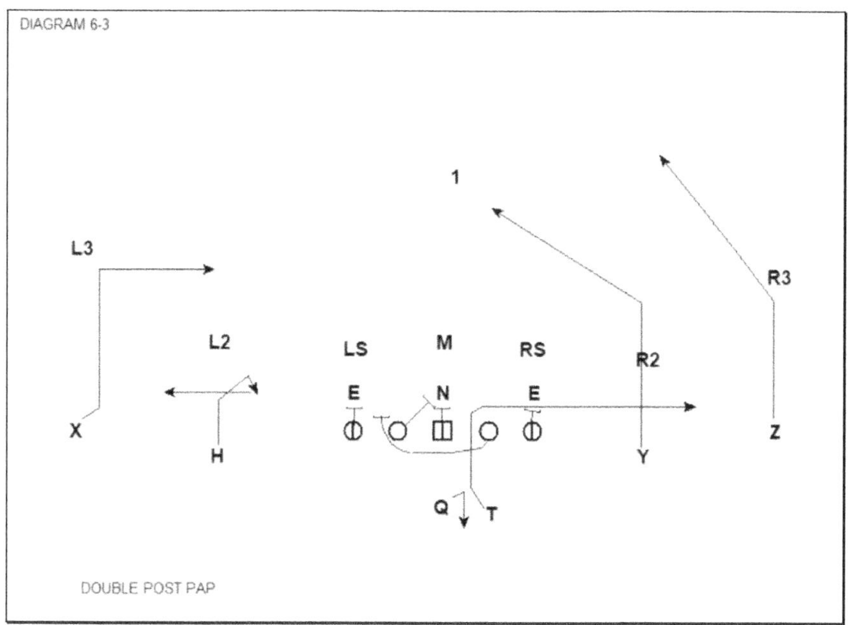

A play caller may also elect to be slightly more conservative when he starts out a P and 10 drive.

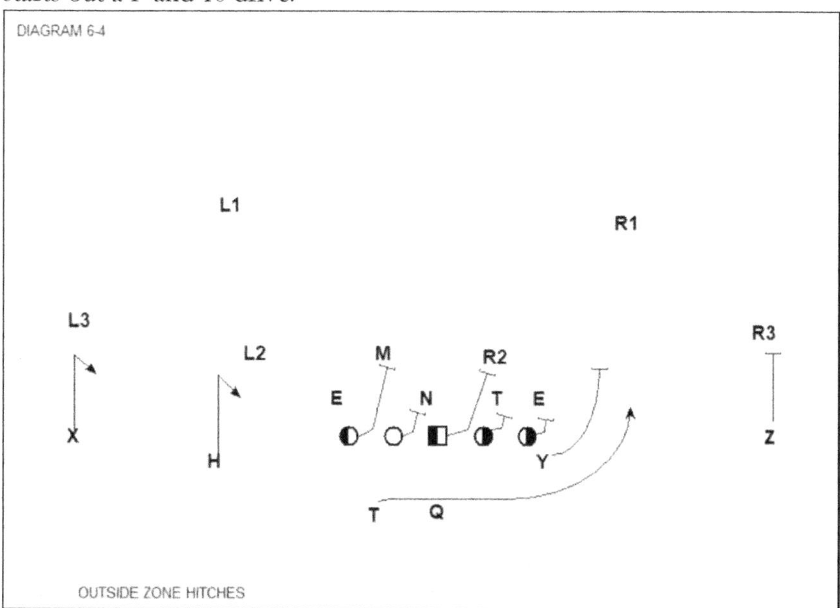

A commonly called RPO play maybe the more appropriate way to start one of these drives. The reason that an RPO might be more effective way to start the drive may be that the play-caller simply is not quite sure what the defense is attempting to do at the start of this possession and therefore he can call a play that has both a run and a pass component that allows the quarterback to read his way out of the situation (Diagram 6-4).

Sometimes an RPO is the best way to attack a defense in a P and 10 situations because it gives the play-caller the greatest amount of flexibility in getting the right play called against a defense. If the play-caller does not feel like he has a good grasp of what the defense will do at the start of this possession it is preferable that the offense start out in an RPO setting. If, however the play-caller feels like he knows what the defense might be attempting to do one of the previously discussed plays might be more advantageous.

Conclusion

As we discussed previously a P and 10 possession is the first possession of any drive in a football game. Often the first possession of a drive is a great tone-setter for what the rest of the drive will look like. And offensive play-caller should take care to make sure that this first set of downs is highly successful in order to set a precedent and a trend for how the rest of that possession will play out. It is essential that the play caller not allow the defense to gain an upper hand in terms of what the structure of the first few plays will look like nor allow the defense to dictate the style of play that will be utilized throughout that possession of downs.

The play caller must take specific care to decide whether he has a good enough grasp of the defense to call a drop-back pass, a quick pass play, a PAP play, or even an RPO. The play caller must take further care to basically attempt to think one step ahead of what the defense is attempting to accomplish. Some defenses are going to attempt to bring pressure and put the offense behind the chains while other defenses are going to drop seven or eight defenders into a zone coverage and attempt to play conservative and keep the ball in front of them. A good offensive coordinator must make this assessment as he is receiving the possession, which sometimes will come in the form of a punt and allow him extra time to prepare but could just as easily come in the form of a defensive turnover which will provide him only a few seconds to prepare. It is essential that the play caller knows what the best way is to come out for this new possession.

It should be game-planned throughout the week what the coach should like to do during a P and 10 situations. However, as the game progresses, these situations will change and morph at an incredibly fast rate and an offensive coordinator must be prepared to be flexible and adjust with these changes as they present themselves inside the atmosphere of play calling on the night of the game.

7
1ST & 10

1st and 10 is important for a variety of reasons. We are looking here not at the first possession of the drive, which is a P and 10 situations, but the first time the offense achieves a 1st down after taking possession of the ball. The 1st and 10 call is of critical importance because it sets the table for whether the offense is likely to achieve a another 1st and 10 situations. RPO based offenses score large amounts of points but one of the major reasons this is true is because these styles of offense can generate large numbers of 1st Downs.

It is a primary philosophical belief in the Surface to Air System that the offense avoiding 3rd Downs is a critical piece of the puzzle in being successful. It is our belief that many defenses will be much more successful on 3rd Down than they will be on First Down. Defenses have a plethora of answers that they can utilize to attack offenses once they have the offense pinned into a 3rd Down situation especially 3rd and Long. If the offense can stay on 1st Down and 2nd Down for most of the game it is our belief that our odds of being successful, scoring points, and winning games is much higher.

It is our belief that 80% of the snaps in each season need to be on 1st or 2nd Down with 19% or less of our snaps coming on 3rd Down. It makes it hypercritical then that the offense on 1st and 10 can get back to another 1st and 10 as quickly as is possible. It then allows that the plays that you call on 1st and 10 are very critical to your overall success. If you call good plays on 1st and 10 then you give yourself a high probability of achieving another 1st Down when this philosophical belief can be practiced and maintained.

Therefore, the number one goal of a Surface to Air System offense on 1st and 10 is to get 5 yards or more every time a play call is made. This means that all the plays that a coach calls on 1st and 10 should be designed to get 5 yards or more at a minimum. While scoring touchdowns is great and might come from time to time on 1st and 10 this is not the overall expressed goal of the offense on this down and distance. A coach might elect to take a shot from time to time in this instance, but the philosophical approach of the system is to put we in position to move the chains. This leads to a frustrated and reactive defense that will likely make large numbers of mistakes and thereby enable the offense to take his chances later in the drive.

If the offense is routinely stalling and not gaining yardage then the defense is able to expand its playbook and eventually gain the upper hand in the contest. If the offensive coordinator can get 5 yards or more on 1st Down the odds are increasingly likely that the coach will be able to get the ball matriculated down the field and score more points.

<u>1st and 10 Plays</u>

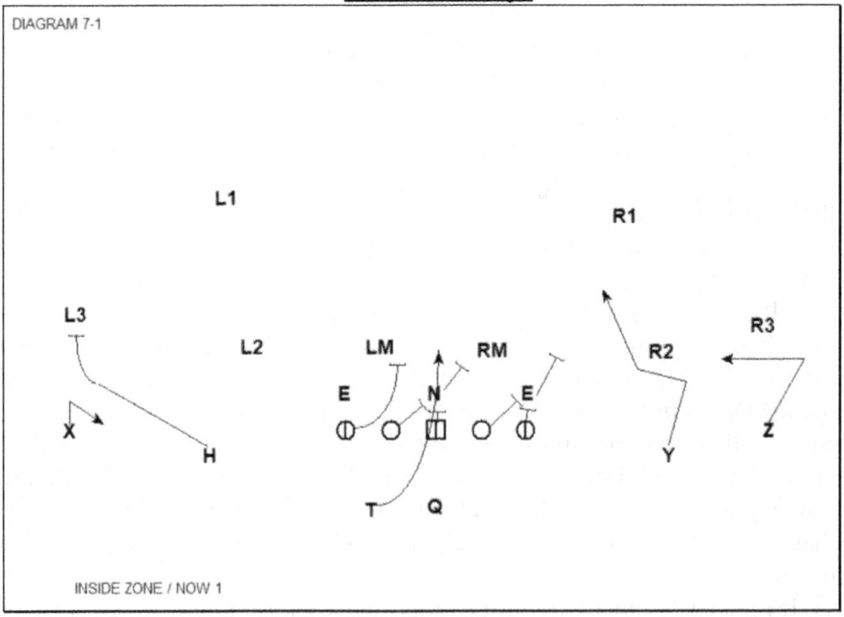

DIAGRAM 7-1

INSIDE ZONE / NOW 1

An offensive coordinator should not take a conservative or passive response to a 1st and 10 call. He should take the approach that he should be aggressive to be successful. The goal of getting 5 yards on 1st and 10 does not mean he should just hand the ball off and hope for the best. It does, however, mean that a heavy reliance on RPOs that have a proven track record of success should be the order of the day.

In the Surface to Air System we feel that increased options give the quarterback more ways to attack the defense and an increased likelihood of putting you, the play caller, in an advantageous position. One way to do this is to stay in a 2x2 structure and call an inside zone with Grass Slants to one side and a Now Screen to the other side (Diagram 7-1).

This sort of play allows the quarterback to have three pre-snap options as well as three more post-snap options for a grand total of six different places to go with the football. This sort of flexibility allows the quarterback to get the ball into places where the defense is most vulnerable and give you a higher probability of calling a play that will get 5 yards and keep your offensive philosophy on track. The quarterback always has the flexibility to change the front door side (the side the run is called towards) on all Surface to Air System RPOs which enhances further his flexibility in making sure the offense gains at least 5 yards. If this is stressed and coached to the quarterback, then he will become highly proficient at making sure the offense remains on target on the 1st and 10 goals you have set for him and the offense.

A second great RPO to remain on schedule on 1st and 10 is to operate from a 3x1 formation to the field and call inside zone with a Bubble Screen attached to the #3 receiver (Diagram 7-2).

DIAGRAM 7-2

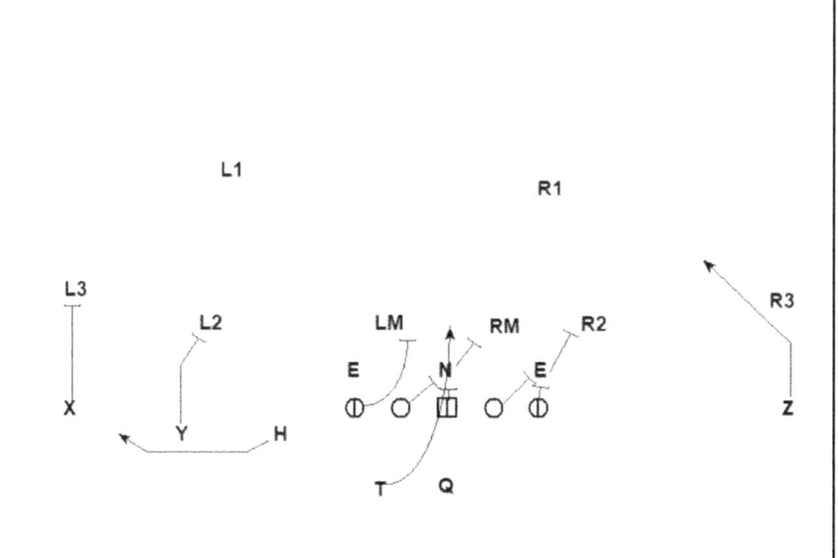

INSIDE ZONE / #3 BUBBLE

This RPO features two pre-snap options and three post-snap options but has the benefit that it allows the offense to stretch the defense to the field. The defense is forced to determine whether they have an R3 that can cover the single side receiver in man coverage or else give up a numbers advantage in the box or to the 3x1 side of the formation. Of course, the offense can elect to play Cover 0 pressure here, but the variety of defense won't do so on 1st and 10 and certainly won't do so if the offense shows it can mix in other man beating types of answers.

A great third option for a 1st and 10 call is to leave the offense in a 2x2 set and call a locked inside zone where the 5 technique is accounted for instead of being read. The offense can then execute Grass Routes to both the front as well as the back-door side of the RPO and place the defense in a variety of matchup and leverage conflicts all at once (Diagram 7-3).

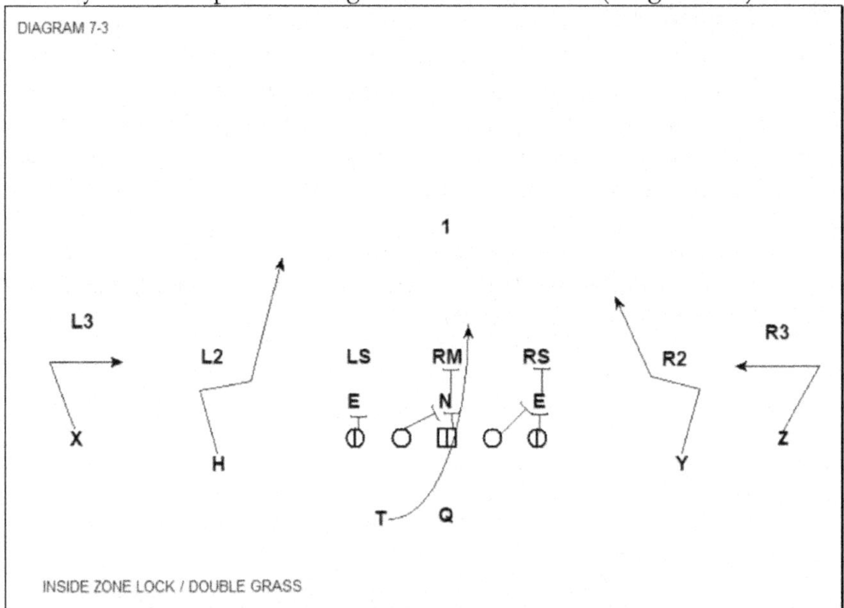

The nature of these routes forces the defense to either devalue the box with two high safeties or face the realization that the offense will attack four defensive backs simultaneously with man coverage beating routes with large areas to potentially run after the catch. This RPO with its route combinations is good versus almost every coverage and or stunt the defense might elect to use and again gives the quarterback a great deal of flexibility to throw a pass or hand the ball of into a box that invites a gain or 5 yards or more.

An offensive coordinator might elect to throw drop back passes on 1st and 10 rather than entering the RPO world. If he does so then executing 4 verticals from a 3x1 set with a crossing route by the X receiver and a Wheel Route by the tailback is a great way to do so (Diagram 7-4).

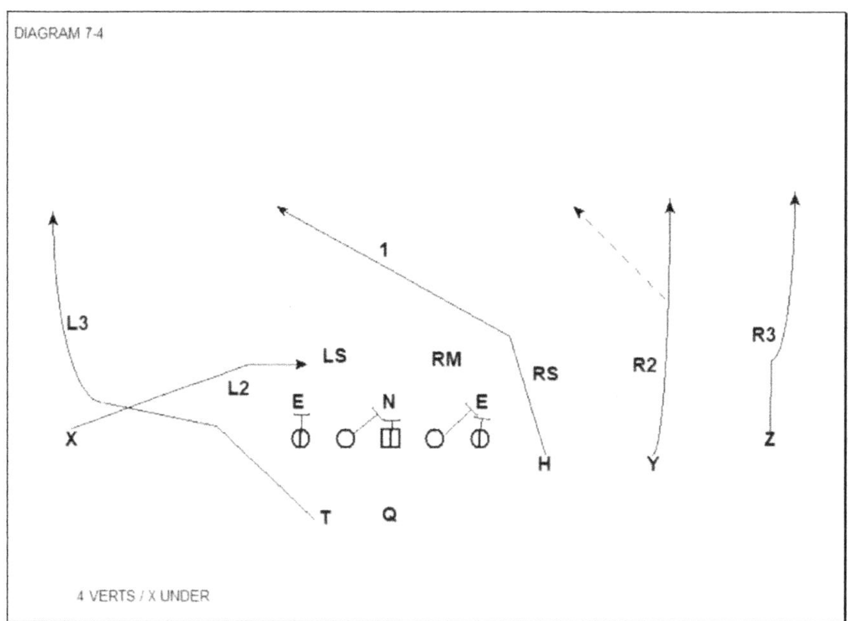

4 verticals from this set allows the offense to stress the defense out across the entire width of the field. This play also allows the quarterback to have the option of attacking man coverage with both the crossing route and the Wheel Route by the tailback.

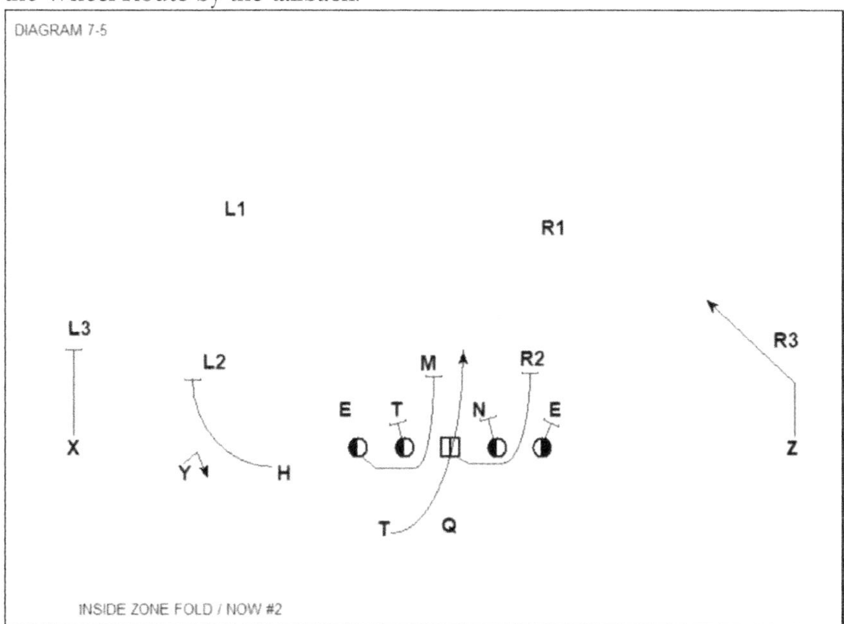

This is not a play that should be called too often on 1st and 10 but it is an option if the play caller feels the defense is too far into either extreme of either bringing pressure or dropping too many defenders into pass coverage zones. This can also be a great way to get a cheap touchdown if the defense has been lulled to sleep with too many quick calls and RPOs on previous 1st and 10 calls.

Film study will oftentimes show certain tendencies from defensive coaches that can aid play calling on 1st and 10. Let's say that the defense always sets their 3 technique to the tailback and or to the 3x1 side of the formation. The play caller can take advantage of this sort of defensive tendency by calling a double fold inside zone scheme that is designed to be executed towards the shade or 1 technique of the defense (Diagram 7-5).

This sort of play calling helps to meld the run and then pass into an RPO, but it also takes advantage of film study and defensive tendencies. This sort of play call can cause the defense to rethink their 1st and 10 structural alignment, which might lead to confusion on the defense, or it will allow you to go back to the same well repeatedly to gain 5 yards using the same formation but different run calls.

Conclusion

1st and 10 is a critical down of football in the Surface to Air System. If this down does not gain 5 yards or more then the likelihood is that the defense will gain an upper hand on 2nd Down and then be able to expand its coverage and blitz package. If the defense can do this then it also expands the likelihood that they can either force a turnover or stop the offense on a 3rd Down play. It is critical that the offense is designed and call to be successful on 1st and 10. I have long maintained the best way for the offense to win on 3rd Down is to simply refuse to play that down. If the play calling is done well on 1st and 10 then perhaps the offense won't have to call 3rd Down plays and thereby reduce the size of the defensive playbook they are facing.

It is essential that a well-informed offensive coordinator build and then call plays that are designed to get the chains moving and keep the offense on schedule. That schedule, as previously mentioned, is 5 yards on 1st and 10. If the offense must change formations, use motion, use shifts, or call certain plays to accomplish this then that is what they should do.

I do not know, nor have I ever felt, that spread offenses can win games where they spend large amounts of time on 3rd Down. Defenses are too good and too multiple when they can win by making a stop one time on one down such as 3rd Down. When the distance on 3rd Down is long then simply creates even more advantages and even more schemes that the defense can utilize. If the offense is successful on 1st and 10 and makes the 2nd Down play short and easier to convert, then they have seriously reduced the defense's answers on this down and increased their own likelihood of generating a 1st Down. An offense that goes in a pattern of 1st and 2nd Downs will have a high probability of scoring points. In short, 1st Downs lead to touchdowns and then game should be called with this axiom in mind on every possession.

8
2ND & SHORT

If 1st and 10 is important, it is important because the offense wishes to get into 2nd Down and short which is defined as 2nd and 5 yards or less to convert a 1st Down. Once the offense has been successful on 1st and 10 it is critical that they accomplish their expressed goal of converting the 2nd Down and short yardage into a 1st and 10 situations. If the defense can stop the offense from achieving this goal, then they will have put the offense back into a 3rd Down situation that is not advantageous for the offense.

The 2nd and Short play is then of critical importance for the offensive play caller to make an accurate decision and ensure that this advantage down is converted quickly in the offense's favor. The play caller should make sure that he calls a play that quickly convert the yardage needed and places the offense back into 1st and 10 and allows the play caller the option of using tempo and moving quickly. Most tempo situations develop naturally as a result of a 1st Down that gains 5 yards and a quick and accurate 2nd and Short decision that converts. Therefore, this down is critical to the offense's success and great care should be taken in calling these plays effectively.

2nd and Short Plays

The 2016 and 2017 self-scout analysis tells us that this section is almost exclusively filled with simple and easy to read RPOs in order to convert the needed yardage. The play caller needs to analyze the box and determine which RPO and which run is best designed to attack the defense in question. In 2016, we saw a great deal of 3-4 fronts paired with a quarters coverage look behind it. An easy answer versus this defense is to call an inside zone and then a Snag Concept to the perimeter (Diagram 8-1).

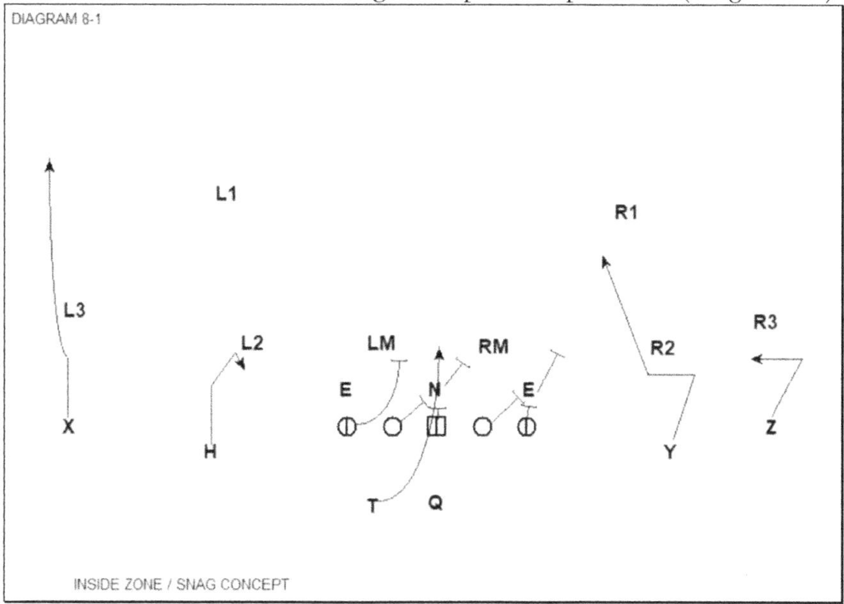

The defense, which only plays five men in the box, is forced to either allow the L2 or the R2 to come off their coverage assignment and add an extra hat to the box in order to stop the run. If neither the L2 nor the R2 comes into the box, then the offense has a favorable run box and a great opportunity to hand the ball off and gain the needed five yards.

If, however, the defense allows one of their flat players to invade the box, the quarterback will have two easily executed RPO throws to destroy that shift and accomplish the same goal of converting the needed yardage by virtue of the pass. This sort of RPO has been highly successful against standard five-man box defenses over the past two seasons. The offensive play caller can stay with the inside zone in this instance or could use a Long Trap or a One Back Power. Any interior based run from this set, versus this box, gives the offense an easy read and a high probability of success in converting.

The Surface to Air System has also had a great deal of success staying in that 2x2 set but having the Y receiver be a sniffer to the wide side of the field. When the offense gets into this set a simple and effective answer, especially against four-man front defenses, has been to execute a split inside zone with the Bubble Screen coming out the back door of the formation (Diagram 8-2).

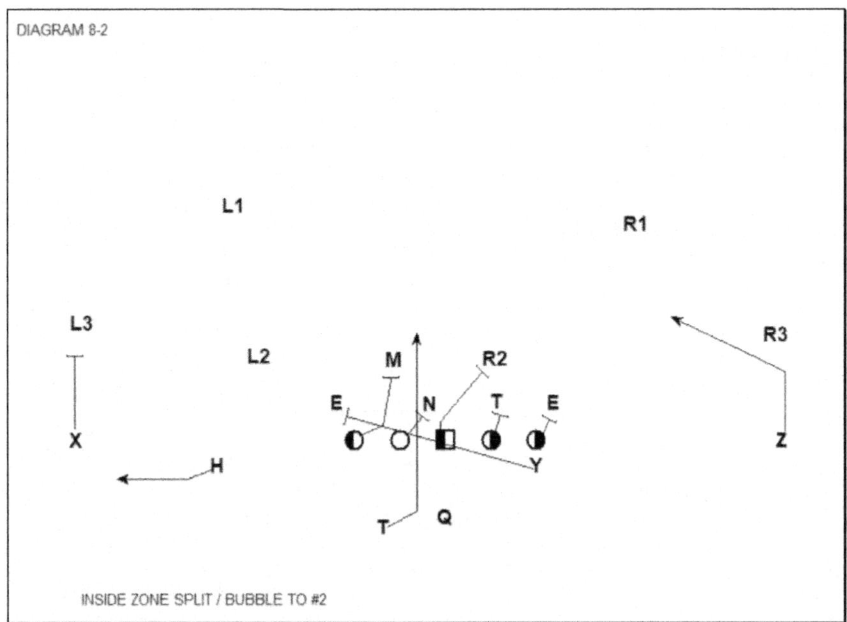

This RPO has the front door Grass Concept and the Bubble Screen as pre-snap options and the quarterback can hand the ball into the box should the defense remain in a 6-man box. The offensive lineman and the Y receiver can account for all the defenders in the box and if the L2 plays into the box then he is replaced post snap with the Bubble Screen throw by the quarterback. This is a simple and low risk play that gives the offense a high probability of converting four to six yards which makes it an ideal call for 2nd Down and Short.

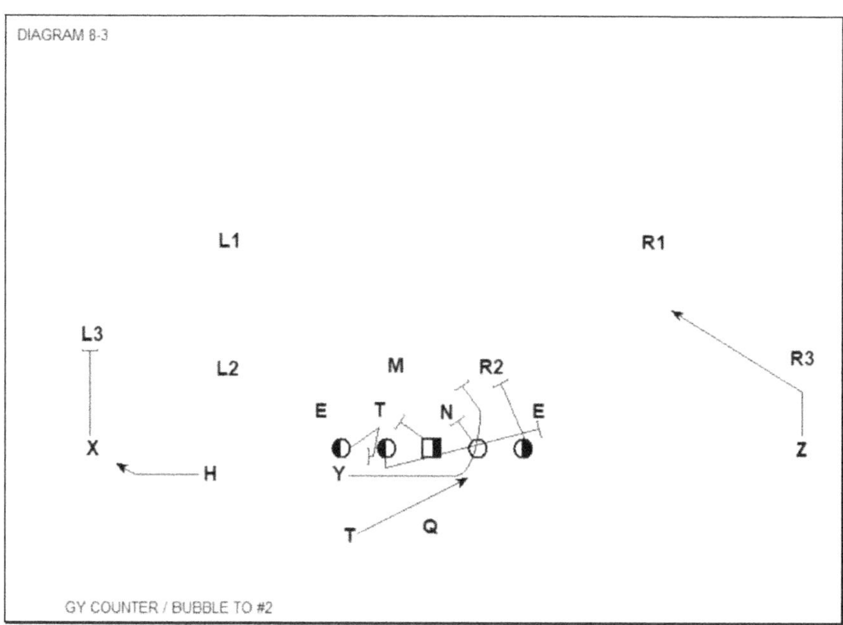

The Surface to Air System is a multi-dimensional offense that can strike the defense from a host of angles and locations. The use of the GY Counter away from a 3x1 sniffer set with an attached Bubble Screen is a very distinct advantage for the offense (Diagram 8-3).

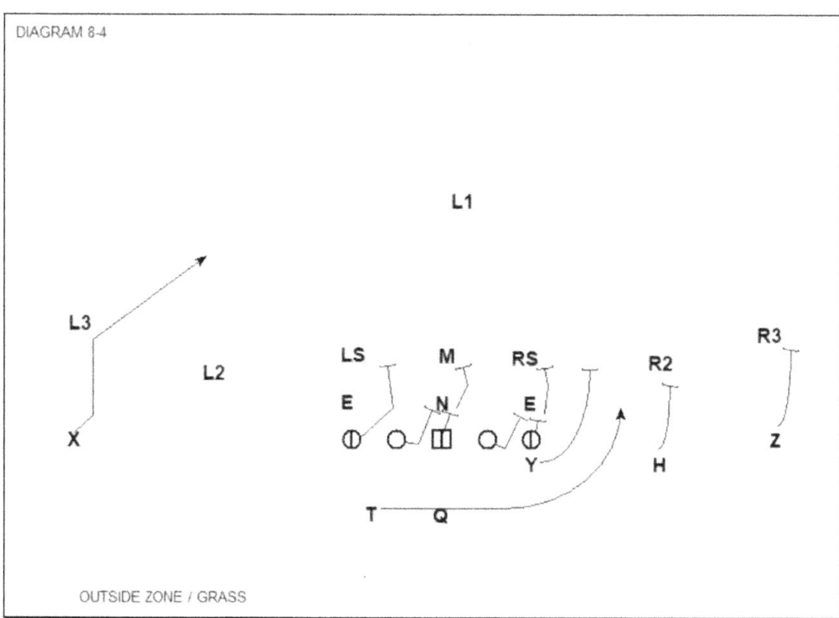

This look allows the offense to lock or unlock the defensive end and forces the defense to play seven defenders in the box or else the offense will have a clean handoff with a numerical superiority inside the box. If the defense attempts to add that seventh man to the box, they will very likely give up and easy throw on the pass portion of the RPO. This play is another tried and true way to get five yards and move the chains once the offense has made it to 2nd Down and is within five yards of a conversion.

A fourth tested answer on 2nd and Short is to utilize a 3x1 sniffer tight end set and run outside zone to the sniffer side of the formation while keeping a Grass Concept on the back-door side (Diagram 8-4).

The defense cannot add defenders to the 3x1 side without giving up and easy Slant Route to the back-door side of the formation. If the defense maintains two defenders to the back-door side, then the offense has a numerical superiority on the 3x1 edge of the defense and can likely achieve the needed five yards before the free safety can arrive on the scene to balance out the numbers for the defense. This sort of RPO is a classic and simple answer to a short yardage problem for the Surface to Air System.

Conclusion

The major priority of the offense is to maintain possession of the football so achieving 1st Downs is a critical component of that strategy. For the offense to maintain the ball they must make five yards or more on 1st and 10 and thereby utilize 2nd Down and Short to convert the chains and gain a fresh set of downs. It has been our experience, that utilizing a wide variety of run calls, with a correspondingly simple set of pass plays is the best way to achieve that goal. The use of simple and highly repeatable RPOs is a preferred way to attack defenses once they have been pushed back on 1st and 10. The offensive play caller should take care to ensure that there is variation in the style of these plays but that they remain simple to execute and simple for the quarterback to read.

9

2ND & MEDIUM

In the S2A System, we define medium as five, six or seven yards. Anything at eight yards to go or longer would fall into the category of long yardage. If the offense failed to gain 5 yards or more then it is in a medium yardage situation. If the offense gained exactly five yards, then it would be up to the play caller to determine if that is a short or medium yardage situation. We define five yards or less to go as short yardage because we want the quarterback to feel he can hand the ball off on five yards or less and feel good about that decision. If the yardage is at five yards to seven yards, then it is a medium situation with a new set of parameters.

The goal of 2nd Down and Medium is that the offense is attempting to get the yardage down to 3rd Down and Short. The offense is attempting to get the ball into a 3rd Down situation that can offer at least a partially favorable chance of converting. If the 1st Down is achieved that is great but the philosophical goal is simply to reduce the distance to go to a manageable amount. The key here is that the defense realizes the offense will be tempted to try and get the entire distance all at once.

For example, if the offense has a 2nd Down and 7 situation the defense will defend as if they know the goal is to attain seven yards. If the offense is simply attempting to get four or five yards, then the defense is likely to allow this to happen. Oftentimes the offense will hand the ball off or throw a short pass and the result will be a seven- or eight-yard gain and the offense will achieve a 1st Down "without trying to do so." This down should not be a conservative down it should be a realistic and relevant down. The offensive coordinator should release he does not have to throw a ball seven yards to achieve a seven-yard gain. The fact that the offense creates a positive momentum play will often result in a 1st Down.

2nd and Medium Plays

As was previously stated, the goal of a 2nd and Medium play is to get the offense to a 3rd Down and Short situation. Most of the plays in this section will again focus on simple RPOs. All these plays are designed to give either the tailback or the receivers to have expanded run after the catch opportunities to gain a minimum number of yards. These plays are also designed to give these athletes a chance to gain extra yardage and perhaps actually gain the 1st Down yardage.

The first play to utilize is a 3x1 sniffer tight end set and run the outside zone play to the field side of the formation (Diagram 9-1).

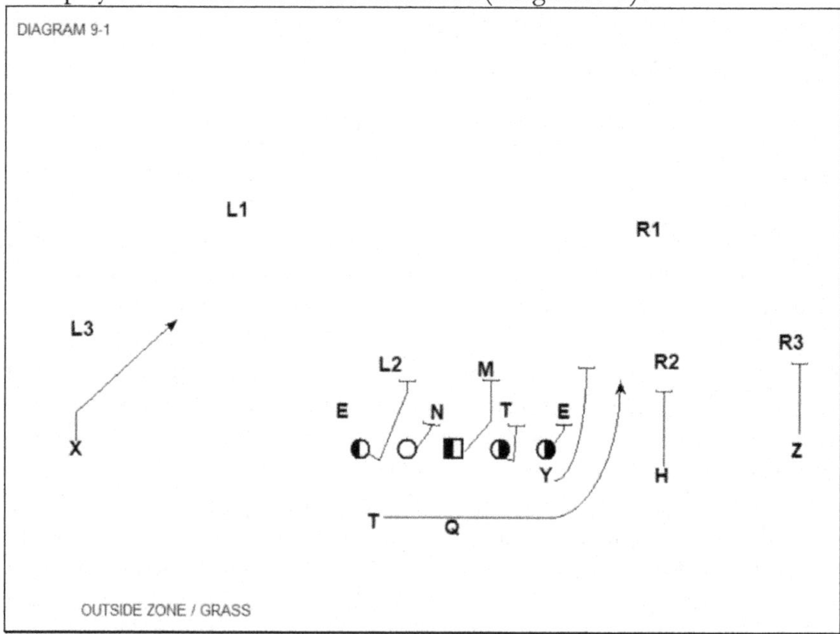

This play features the Grass Concept Slant Route on the back door of the play so that the offense has the option to throw for a first down or at least hold two defenders. The outside zone to the field side gives the tailback the option to circle the field or cut into the line of scrimmage and make a read based upon where the defense is playing.

Another great way to utilize outside zone is to execute the outside zone play towards the sniffer tight end side of the formation with a 2x2 formation (Diagram 9-2).

This play allows the offense to play balanced against a standard 4-2-5 defense and force them to decide whether to place their fifth defensive back either to the sniffer side of the formation or to the two-receiver side of the formation.

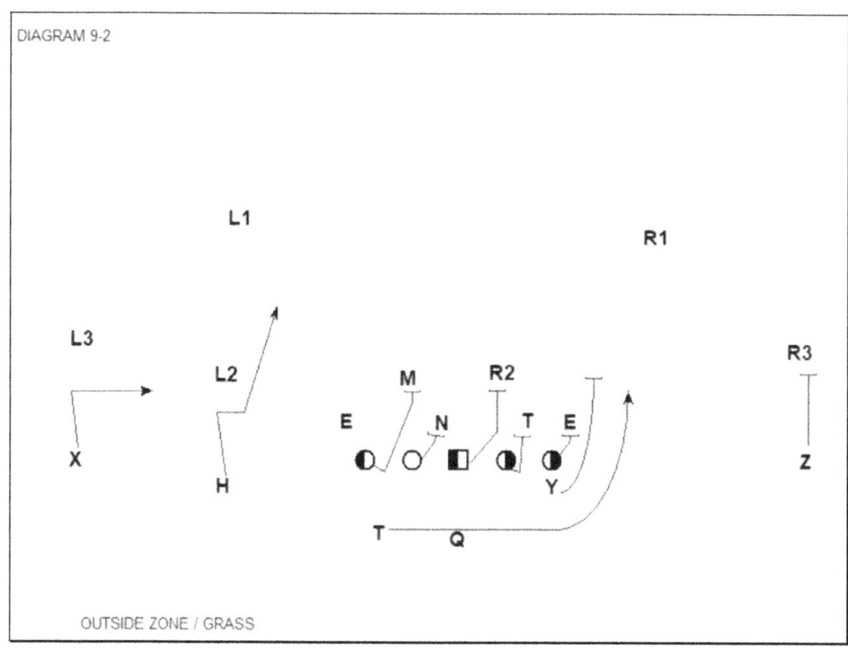

This compels an unbalanced defense, like the 4-2-5, to decide where to slide this fifth defensive back to one side of the play or the other and allows the quarterback to read that player and make the offense correct. This structure is advantageous in that it forces the defense to remain balanced. These first two plays are essentially mirror images of one another but attack different defenses and different structures.

If the defense is a more balanced structure like a 3-4 Defense, then utilizing a 3x1 set if the more preferred formation on this down and distance. The ability to line up in a 3x1 set gives the offense an unbalanced appearance to the defense and forces them to decide where to allocate their resources. If the offense utilizes a gap scheme run such as the 1 Back Power and pairs it with any route to the third receiver, such as a Bubble Screen, this can be an easy and lethal play for the offense (Diagram 9-3).

This play allows the offense to get a man on a man in the box and +1 the defense by adding the tailback to the equation. The quarterback has an easy pre-snap throw to the Bubble Screen receiver if the defense does not run a defender out of the box. Of course, should the defense run a defender out of the box then the quarterback would read him and have an easy conversion for the throw. The defense is almost forced to either give up the easy throw to the H receiver or alter their entire defense for this one play into an unbalanced defense. Most defensive coordinators simply won't change their whole defense for one play and thereby give the offense an opportunity at an easy conversion.

The RPO Game is fundamentally a triple option style of offense in football. The reason that RPOs are so successful is they isolate defenders and put them into conflict especially on the edges of the defense. One such way that modern offenses can put defenses into a great deal of conflict is by inserting the sniffer tight end into the game and then using him in a load option scheme against the edge of the defense. The load option is defined as the sniffer tight end going around the defensive and who is being read and attacking the first linebacker behind him inside the box. This sort of structure prevents the defense from being able to play a squeeze / scrape style of attack and thereby reduces the answers the defense can come up with.

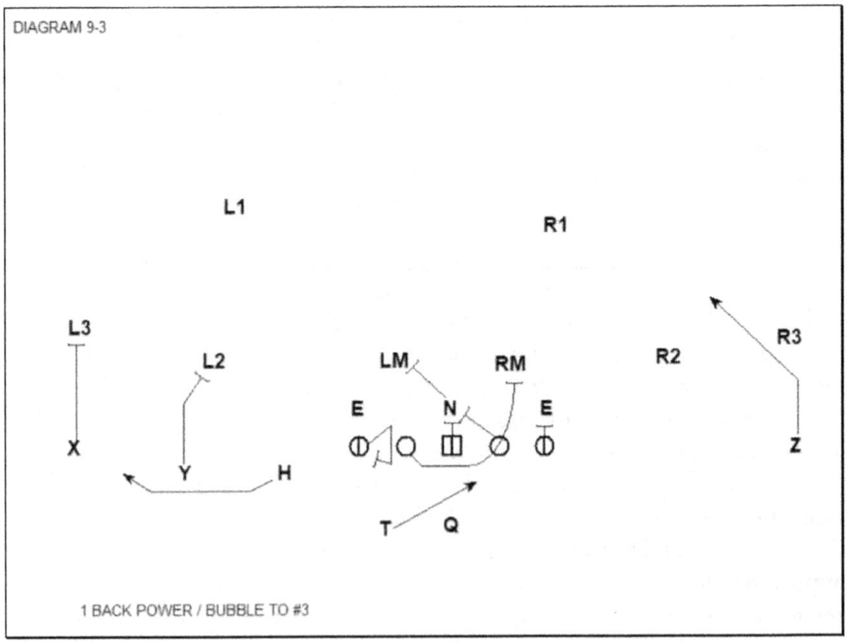

1 BACK POWER / BUBBLE TO #3

The addition of a Bubble Screen onto the back-door side of the this play essentially isolates the defensive end and makes him wrong regardless of how he plays this action (Diagram 9-4).

The defensive end can either take the tailback or feather and play the quarterback. If the ball will be handed off and the offense will have numbers to run the ball. If he crashes and the linebacker attempts to scrape, then the sniffer will account for him and now the L2 player will face the conflict. The L2 cannot cover both the quarterback and the Bubble Screen and so he will be caught two on one and isolated. This sort of RPO is just standard triple option football and has been a staple for us for the past two seasons on 2nd and Medium situations.

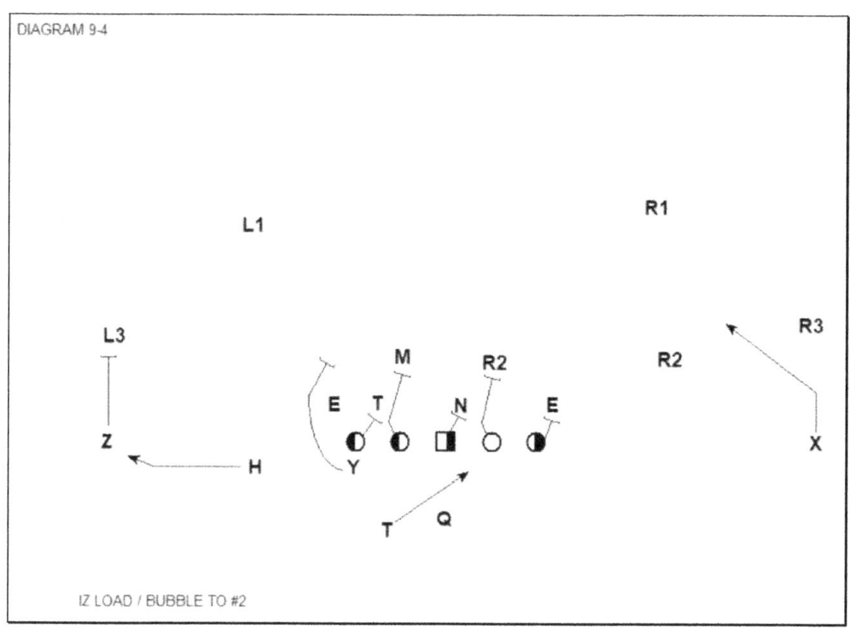

A fifth answer to 2nd Down and Medium might be to block the surface of the defense and throw quick game. Many different types of quick game concepts can be useful, but the key is tempo.

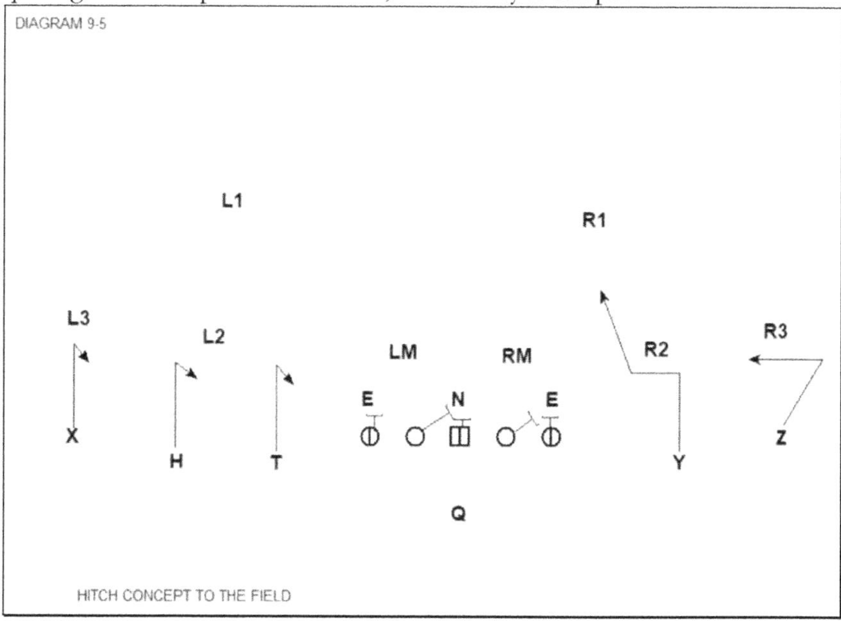

If the defense has trouble lining up after a 1st and 10 call and they are discombobulated, then going to 3x2 and throwing quick game can be an easy way to convert back to 1st and 10. One such concept is to execute triple hitches with a Grass Concept to the opposite side of the formation (Diagram 9-5).

The defense can be explored in that they may not be able to line up to this 3x2 set quickly and therefore they might leave areas of grass vulnerable to attack. The play caller must be cognizant of whether the defense responds quickly to formation changes and how they do so. If the defense makes an easy check to 3x2 then a 3x2 RPO might be in order. However, it has been our experience that many defenses do not process this change quickly enough they will allow one of the receivers to go generally uncovered at the line of scrimmage for a few seconds. It is up to the play caller to recognize this and jump out of the RPO world and simply throw quick passes to achieve a 1st and 10 situation and keep the chains moving.

Conclusion

2nd and Medium is a critical situation for the offense in the modern game of football. The main reason why 2nd and Medium is such a critical play for the offense is because as we stated earlier the offense must avoid 3rd Down situations. If the offense does not avoid 3rd Down situations than it is too easy for the defense to expand their playbook and come up with a multitude of answers to attack the offense's structure. Therefore, the offense must take great care when they are in 2nd and Medium to get themselves to a 3rd and Short situation at a bare minimum. If the offense can get to a 3rd Down and Short situation then it increases the likelihood that the offense will be able to convert.

Many coaches get hyper-aggressive in this situation and attempt to get the entire 1st Down all at once, and I feel that this is a mistake. While it could be true that the offense might get seven or eight yards on 2nd Medium it is a highly more likely situation that the offense will hold the ball longer taking more risks down the field on a drop back pass and lose yardage.

The offense might not be advised to take huge risks and take themselves from 3rd and Short into 3rd and Medium or even 3rd and Long. It should not be said that in modern RPO offenses the coordinator should be conservative, but they should be realistic. This realistic attitude is predicated on the idea that the defense will be willing to give up four to five yards on 2nd Medium but they will not be likely to give up the sticks all at once and give up a 1st Down.

It therefore brings the age-old adage that it is far more likely for the offense to get a quick pass or a run and that receiver or running back get the needed yardage than it is to hold the football and throw it further down the field. 2nd and Medium is a critical down and should be analyzed with care.

10
2ND & LONG

The expressed goal of the Surface to Air System is to gain five yards on 1st and 10. If the offensive coordinator is forced to call plays on 2nd and Long then this philosophy has hit a snag on this series. The offense now faces a 2nd and Long situation which is defined by us as eight yards or further to convert the 1st Down and 10. This situation should be viewed, as all situations in the Surface to Air System should be viewed, as an opportunity for the offense to convert a 1st Down and keep the pressure on the defense.

These situations have caused us to diversify our offensive menu a bit over the last few seasons. In this category we now include RPOs, quick game passes, and drop back passes. This section of the system is very multidimensional because defenses are starting to smell blood in the proverbial waters on a down and distance such as this.

The defense is trained to determine on what towns and distances they are at an advantage and in what situations they are at a disadvantage. A 2nd and Long situation is a down where the defense will likely work to its polar extremes. This means that some defenses will play drop zone coverage that floods the field and keeps the ball in front of them and allows us to have some yardage in exchange for not converting the 1st Down. There is also a defensive philosophy that holds this is a pressure down where the defense can play some man coverage and look at bringing an extra rusher.

The point is that defenses react in a variety of ways on this down and distance as it is the first real situation where they sense they have an opportunity to gain control. A 1st Down call or anything from 2nd and Medium to 2nd and Short is really an advantage still for the offense. Once the chains move to 2nd and Long, the offense still have control of the chains, but that control is beginning to wane. The defense will decide starting here whether they are comfortable playing for space and time or whether they want to force the issue by bringing pressure. This altered tendency, but the defense means the offense needs to begin preparing to challenge the defense in new ways.

The goal of the offense in a 2nd and Long yardage situation is to get half the needed yardage back. If the offense faces a 2nd and * yards to convert, then we are trying to get four yards. This is a standard answer for the quarterback and gives him an easy target to aim for on this slightly more stressful down and distance.

It requires more than just sending the quarterback out there and telling him to make good decisions. He needs to know that if he faces ten yards to convert on 2nd Down he does not have to be a hero and try and get it all at once. When he feels pressured to do too much, he gets sacked or forces balls where they should not be forced. The quarterback needs to know that he can take wheat the defense gives him and attempt to get half the yardage. If he executes and makes a good decision there is a chance that the athlete, he disseminated the ball to might get the needed yardage after the catch or handoff anyway. This sort of thinking eases the quarterback's mentality and makes him an informed decision maker.

2nd and Long Plays

The offense has the capacity to stick with some basic RPOs in this down and distance, but they must take account for the fact that the defense might elect to bring more pressure against these sorts of situations. A great way to invite and then combat this sort of pressure is by playing 3x1 sets to the field. This formation allows the defense to bring pressure more easily if that is their answer but without disguising it well from a boundary to field relationship. A great play to counter any expected pressure with is a Grass Concept from the 3x1 set (Diagram 10-1).

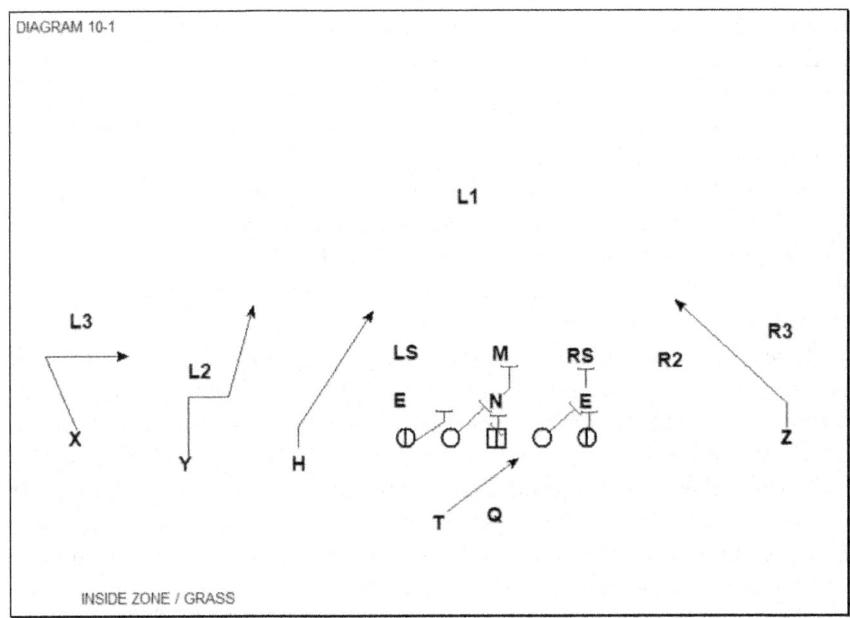

This play has the advantage that it features Slant Routes by four different receivers who can angle into grass areas that are vacated by blitzing linebackers.

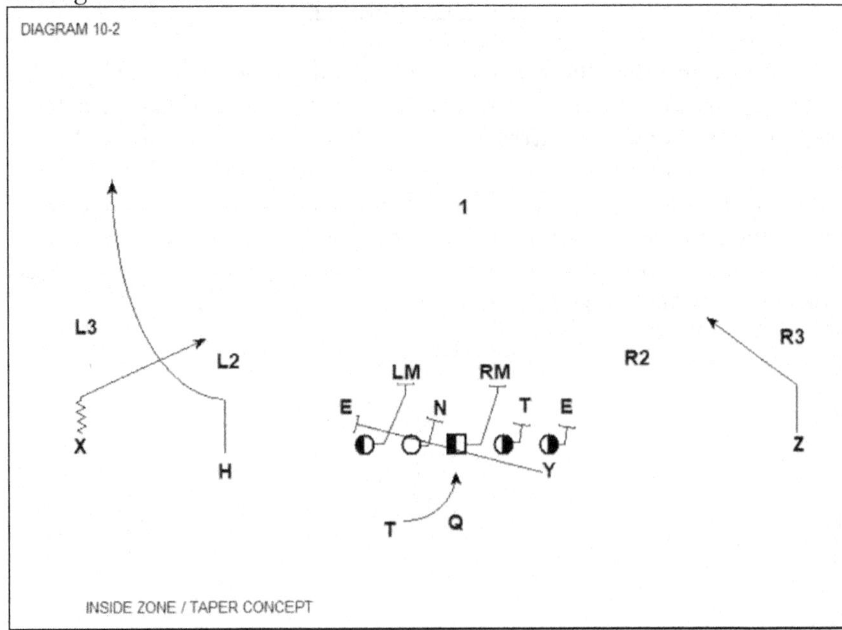

If the defense elects to roll coverage in any meaningful way it is highly likely one of these routes will break into a void and be running wide open for the quarterback to throw to. If, however, the play caller guessed wrong and the defense stayed in base these routes will pull defenders from the box and allow the quarterback to hand the ball into a devalued box and pick up at least half of the needed yardage.

The previous RPO was a standard style of play and very easy to execute by all the parties involved. It was also very conservative and did not involve the offense taking a major risk. It essentially attacked and punished the defense for taking a risk. However, the play caller might elect to take an entirely different approach and push the envelope with a man coverage beating RPO. If the play caller feels that the defense will play some sort of Cover 1 defense and take a risk adding defenders into the box, then he can counter this action with a split inside zone Taper Fade RPO concept (Diagram 10-2).

This RPO features inside zone with a sniffer executing a split zone action that enables the quarterback to count the box. If the defense is playing man coverage, then they will likely have added a defender to the box and be keying the run to stop the offense from gaining any additional yardage. The defense has chosen to be aggressive by pre-snap look and has invited a Cover 1 beating concept like the Taper Fade Concept.

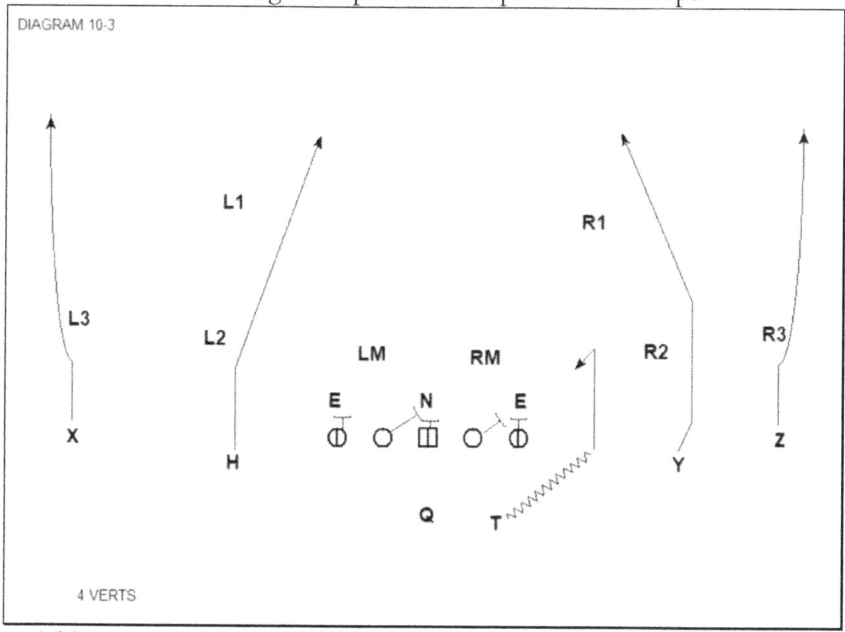

This route structure allows both the split end and the slot receiver to win and aids them with a natural "rub" of their routes. As the defense has added seven men to the box and equated numbers there, they have devalued their secondary and allowed one on one opportunities for the offense to exploit. The quarterback may take the Stutter Slant Route for an easy gain or go over the top for the big play with the Taper Route. These sorts of play call keep the quarterback in an RPO world but offers a uniquely aggressive version of this style of play.

If the play caller feels he must get into a drop back situation to convert the 1st Down, then it is preferable to stick with the 4 Verticals Concept as it spreads the field very effectively. A great way to do this is to add motion with the tailback out of the box so that the defense must declare their intentions to play man or zone coverage (Diagram 10-3).

The route that the tailback runs is up to the play caller and what sort of attachment he thinks he will see from the linebacker against that player. The purpose of the motion simply is to tip the defense's hand and make them declare a coverage for the quarterback pre-snap. Once the coverage is identified the quarterback will find it much easier to find the matchup that is best for him and make an accurate decision and corresponding throw.

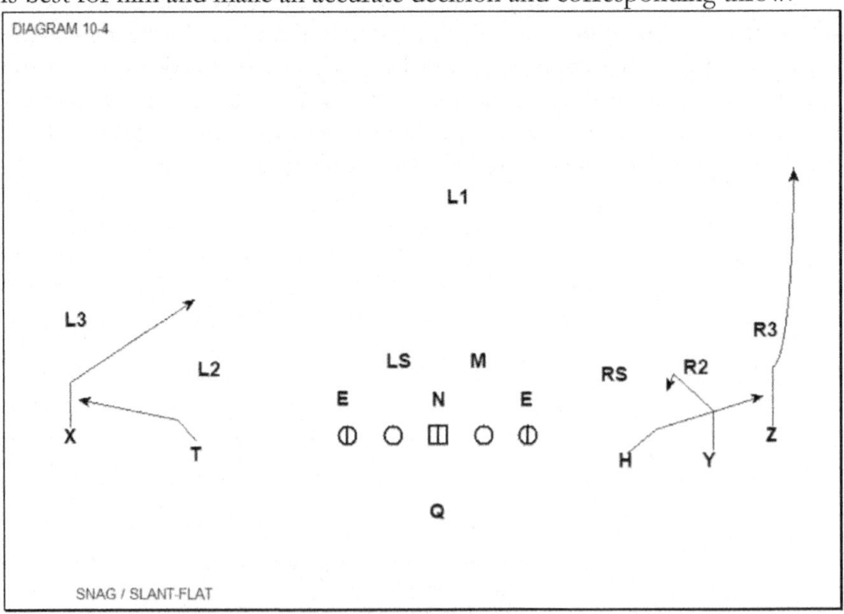

Another equally plausible solution to 2nd and Long for us over the past few seasons has been to pass set the offensive lineman and throw quick game concepts that are not mirrored to both side of the formation. This is, once again, a way to control the face of the defense and make them declare their intentions.

Many defenses have checks for 3x2 sets that force them to alter their basic intentions that were called from the sideline. It is our belief that when the defense is forced to make checks they are often discombobulated and more easily taken advantage of because the defensive coordinator has less control of events. A great play to call in this instance is a Snag Concept to the field and a Slant Flat Concept to the boundary (Diagram 10-4).

This concept is useful because the Snag Concept attacks most two high safety families of coverages. The Slant Flat Concept effectively attacks any sort of Cover 1 or Cover 0 type of coverage look. When these two concepts are paired together, they make for easy answers to both side of the field regardless of what the quarterback is facing when he comes to the line of scrimmage. This sort of quick pass concept makes for a high probability of success that the quarterback can get a completion and makeup at least half of the needed yardage.

The fifth and final play in this chapter is a bit unconventional but highly effective if the offense is facing a pressure-based defense or a highly conservative defense but does not want to risk throwing the football. The play is an outside zone blocking scheme for the offensive lineman with the quarterback executing a wide speed option against the first defender outside the defensive end (Diagram 10-5).

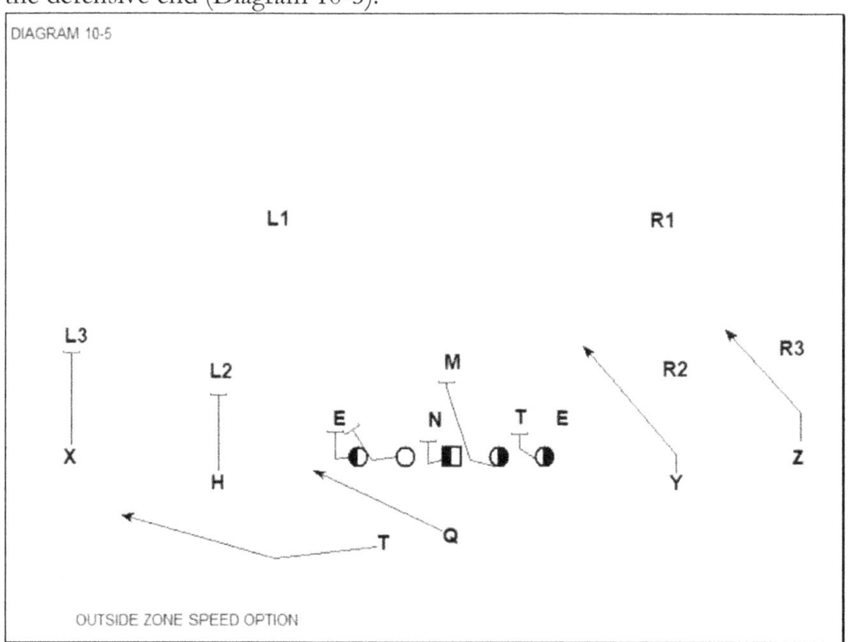

This play will be a great way to attack any pressure man defenses because the pressure will be accounted for with the sliding offensive lineman and any outside blitz would be pitched off by the quarterback. If the defense is playing any sort of base defense, then the likelihood is that the quarterback will essentially run quarterback sweep and keep the ball for at least a modest gain. This is an easy play to call on 2nd and Long because it meets the criteria of likely picking up at least half the yardage needed regardless of what sort of defensive posture the opposition chooses to play.

Conclusion

When the defense can successfully put the offense in a 2nd Down and Long situation they will many times feel like they have achieved a victory. It is up to the offense to ensure that this victory is short-lived and that they begin to reacquire yardage as quickly as possible. It should be the fundamental goal of the offense to gain at least half of the needed yardage anytime they are in a 2nd Down and Long situation. It is critical that the offensive play caller not call overly risky plays that increase the chances of a turnover or a loss of yardage.

It should be remembered that sometimes punting is an acceptable alternative to taking undue risk. However, it is not the goal of any offense to punt and so the play caller should assess what the defense is attempting to do in these situations. If the defense is either overly aggressive or overly passive, then there are corresponding plays that were discussed in this chapter that can be utilized.

An informed offensive play caller will assess and evaluate what the defense is doing in these situations and call plays that offer a high probability of success. The play caller should not be overly risky on these downs but should not be a conservative either. These are opportunities to be successful and even score but they are opportunities that must be assessed and reflected upon and the correct type of plays must be utilized.

Above all, it is critical that the quarterback is coached to understand that his job is to get half the needed yardage. It should be added that once the quarterback understands his role, he should also be told to never pass up the opportunity for a big play should the opportunity present itself. This is a delicate balancing act that must be coached and trained for the play caller to get the results he wishes to see on game nights.

11
3RD & SHORT

Regardless of how the offense got to the situation to be in a 3rd Down and Short position the goal must be to convert the 1st Down. 3rd Down and Short is defined as any distance under five yards. The offense has had two downs by this point to gain at least six yards and make it 3rd Down and less than five yards. The goal of this down is to solidify those gains and finish off moving the chains.

It is critical that the offense not lose this momentum and be forced to punt when they have already gotten themselves into an advantageous position to convert the 1st Down. These plays are designed to give the offense maximum opportunity to convert the 1st Down by changing the style and structure of the plays. If the offense has achieved success on the first two downs utilizing different types of zone plays, then it is necessary to begin adding "window dressing" on this down in order to keep the defense off balance.

These plays will involve new motions and new structures to attempt to gain some sort of small advantage on the defense. This is a critical down, as they all are, because the offense must establish confidence that it can convert to 1st Down every time the distance is less than five yards. It is also critical to put the defense in a position where they feel they won't be successful stopping the offense in these situations and thereby reduce their confidence level. When the defense's confidence level drops, they are much more likely to make mistakes and take risks that are not prudent for them.

3rd Down and Short Plays

The defense has the same realization and the complimentary yet opposite goal of the offense on 3rd Down and Short; to force the offense to punt and stop the conversion of a 1st Down. This is a critical component of any defense. Since the game began, and especially since offenses have evolved into shotgun based spread sets, defenses have made it a priority to be successful on 3rd Down. There have been a host of journal article written about 3rd Down and how defenses will scheme to stop offenses.

I believe that getting five yards or more on 1st and 10 is much more important of a cause for the offense. If the offense gets five yards or more on 1st Down, then they are much less likely to ever get to 3rd Down. In fact, I make it a priority and feel I win more games when my teams don't have to play much on 3rd Down.

However, this chapter is a discussion of what happens once we are there. The defense has the advantage that the play is a 3rd Down call and they must make one stop to win. The offense has the advantage that there are only a few yards needed to convert. The type of plays we select here then must be high probability of success plays that will almost guarantee that we gain positive yardage. As was stated previously, we want these plays to be slightly less conventional and ones that change the status quo of defensive reads.

The first play we have utilized a great deal over the last two seasons is our sniffer tight end insert play. On this play we lock the inside zone and insert the tight end on the back side of the zone in the first open gap (Diagram 11-1).

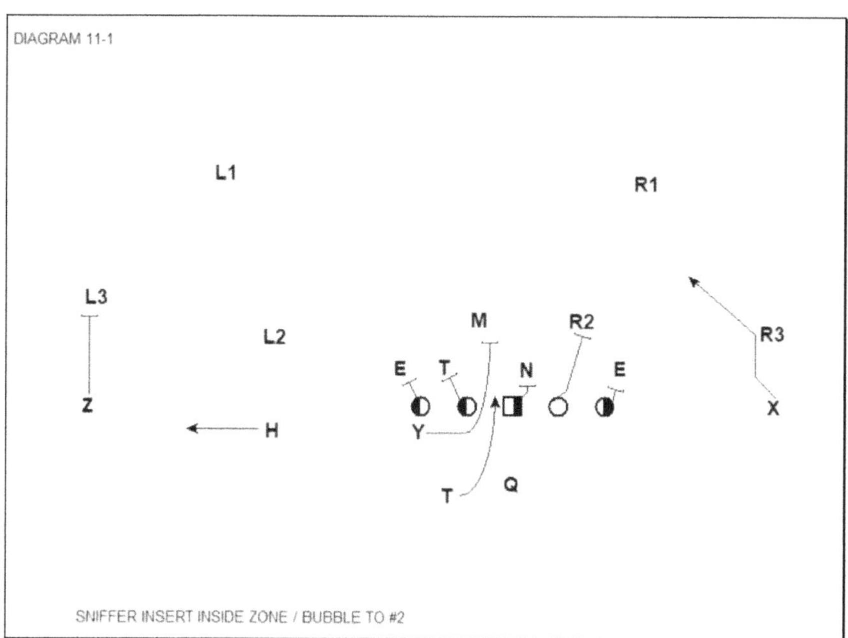

This play essentially establishes the old I formation Isolation Play. The Bubble Screen that is attached to this play and the front door Slant Route keep the defense from adding defenders to the box. If defenders attempt to add to the box, they are read by the quarterback and thrown off accordingly. This type of play allows the offense to play a smash mouth style with a north/south run behind a lead blocker. This is exactly the sort of play that helps the Surface to Air System to achieve 1st Downs in a 3rd Down and Short scenario.

In addition to smash mouth plays, the system utilizes formational tweaks to keep the defense guessing. The use of a 3x1 sniffer set with the tailback removed to create a 3x2 set is just this sort of formational tweak that can disorient a defense. The defense will identify the 3x2 set and likely spread their resources thin across the field to prevent easy throws by the offense. The offense can utilize the outside zone by the offensive lineman but add in the H receiver executing this play as a Jet Sweep (Diagram 11-2).

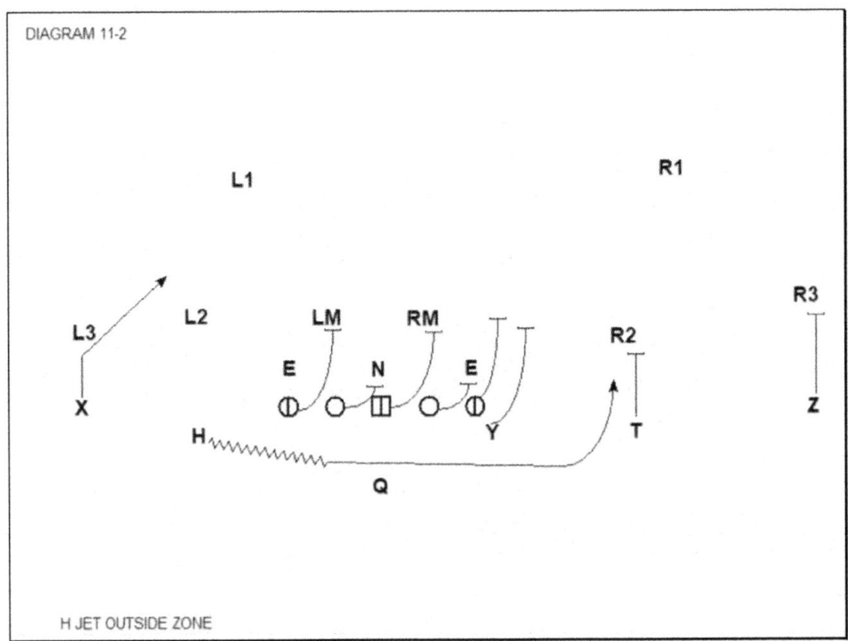

The 3x2 set here forces the defense to extend across the field and allows the offense to execute the Jet Sweep into a three-receiver blocking surface. This sort of play destroys the conventional wisdom that the offense will stay conservative and run the ball right at the defense. It also allows the offense to get the ball into the hands of one of its best playmakers in space. This motion also sets up additional plays that can be utilized on other 3rd Down calls throughout the contest.

Another way to aid the offense in achieving these last few yards to convert is by combining the use of a unique formation and unique motion with an RPO in the same play. In this instance the offense will line up in a 2x2 split back look. The offense will utilize something called Bounce Motion by the H receiver to create a late three receiver surface to the flat (Diagram 11-3).

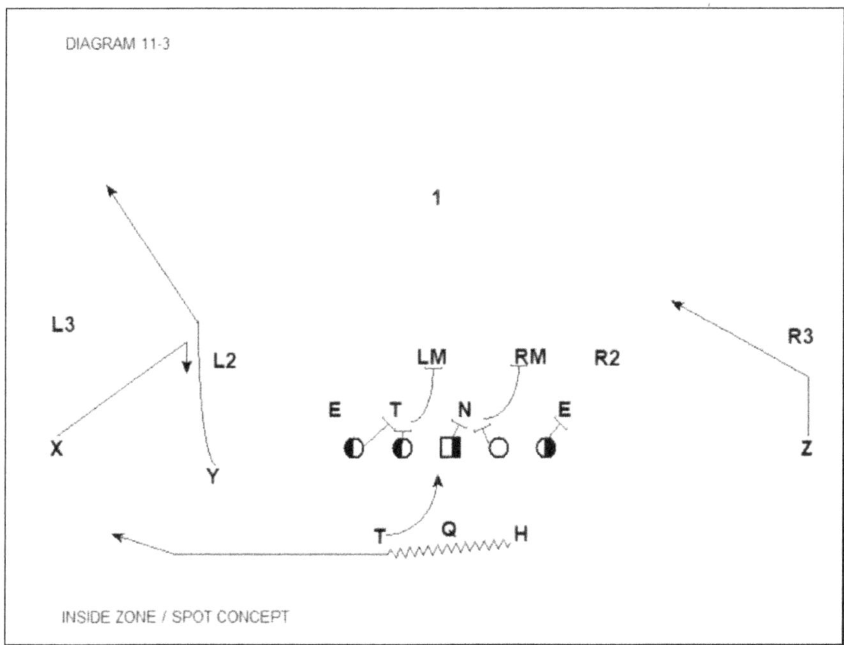

The quarterback can look at the pre-snap Slant Route to the front door side to start with. If he does not like that part of the play the he puts the H receiver in motion and its color leaves the box to chase the motion, he will play zone read football and read his way to a good outcome. If, however, the defense does not chase the motion then the quarterback has a numbers advantage to the flat and should pull the ball and execute the best throw possible to convert. In this instance, the Spot Concept was selected but a three-receiver quick game concept has a high compatibility rate with this sort of RPO.

A fourth commonly used RPO the last two years is a sniffer 3x1 set with 1 Back Power paired with one of our Surface to Air System "S" Calls known to us as Spot (Diagram 11-4).

This is a locked RPO usually because most defenses will play their 3 technique to the sniffer tight end side and make it hard for us to read the defensive end to that side of the play. The 1 Back Power Play is very useful to block five of the six defenders in the box. The sixth defender can then be read by the quarterback on the Pop Pass. The L2 and L3 are prevented from influencing the play that's to the Spot Concept that is called to the perimeter.

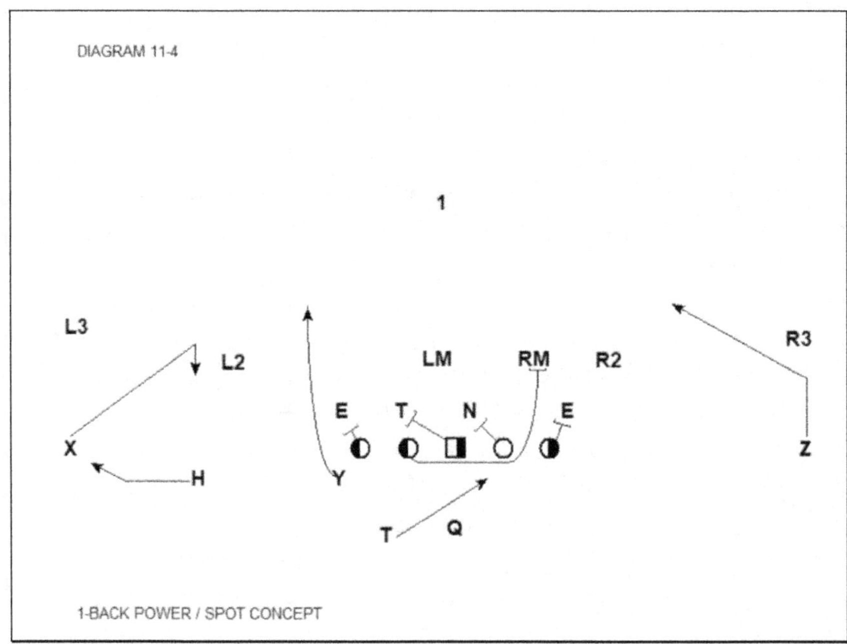

This is an easy play to read for the quarterback and one that lends itself nicely to gaining positive yardage. If the defense elects to focus on the run aspect of the play the Pop Pass will likely pick up the 1st Down. If the defense bails defenders out of the box, then essentially the offense is backing to running an Isolation Play with the guard serving now as the lead blocker.

Conclusion

3rd Down and short is a "money down" for both the offense and the defense in the sense that they are battling to determine if there will be a new set of downs or a turnover. The offense must be proficient in this scenario as it dictates what will happen in the preceding numerical downs of the next series, To put it another way, if an offense is highly successful on 3rd and Short then defenses will have to take more risks on 1st and 2nd Down calls which will allow the offense to call more aggressive and more successful plays when the downs are in their favor.

If the defense feels that the offense will consistently convert on 3rd and Short they will play more man coverage and bring more pressure early in the cycle and the offense will likely get bigger gains on 1st and 10 and maybe even convert 1st Downs on 1st Down. It is my experience that when the offense can progress from 1st Down to 1st Down quickly there is a much greater likelihood that we will score 40 or more points. This down will often require the offense to be creative and not allow the defense to see the same sorts of looks that already gained yardage previously. It is up to the play caller to make sure he uses unique plays here but ones that maintain simple reads where the quarterback is asked to make an easy read and decision to gain the needed yardage. It should be stated; the offense will need to practice these situations and the quarterback needs to know what options in these RPOs give him the best chance of success.

12
3RD & MEDIUM

3rd and Medium is defined as 3rd Down and five to seven yards to go to convert. This is a narrow window because the offense is aware that just one play separates them from having to go for it on 4th Down or punt the football away. This section may sound a bit confusing to the passing observer.

We tell the offense that their goal is to get to 4th and 2 yards to go to convert. We do not talk about converting a 1st Down when the distance is further than five yards to go to convert on 3rd Down. The reason for this is that all the advantages lay with the defense. They can play zone or play man coverage here. They can be aggressive or conservative. We have failed to achieve what we sought out to do on 1st and 2nd Downs and so we do not wish to exacerbate the problem by throwing an interception or taking a sack on a 3rd and Medium or 3rd and Long situational call.

We do not ask the quarterback to attempt to be a "hero" and stand back there and decipher an expanded playbook that the defense is now operating with. This is not to say that we are not trying to convert the 1st Down, quite the contrary, we are hoping that we either hand the football off or throw a quick pass and put the pressure on the defense to make a tackle before we attain the needed yardage. I instruct the offense that if they want me to even consider being aggressive and going for it on 4th Down, they must get the offense into a 4th Down and 2 or less situation. The offense must prove to me as a play caller that they can put us into a manageable situation before we can contemplate the idea of risking a turnover on downs.

The plays that a play caller selects here should then be very specific. We tend to call a high number of simple RPOs that create an equal likelihood of handoffs to quick passes. We do not include much drop back or screens in this area because at 3rd Down and Medium I am still contemplating going for it on 4th Down. I simply want to see success here and get me to a situation where it is a difficult decision for me to make whether to go for it on 4th Down.

3rd Down and Medium Plays

The most common play we are going to call on 3rd and Medium is inside zone because it is simple to call and simple for our players to adjust should the defense give us a crazy look. We are sensitive that as the downs and distances increase the defense controls more of the game and has more coverage and pressure options. We will call a simple slate of RPOs that all base out of an inside zone look. The first RPO we will use is inside zone with a Spot Concept from a 2x2 structure (Diagram 12-1).

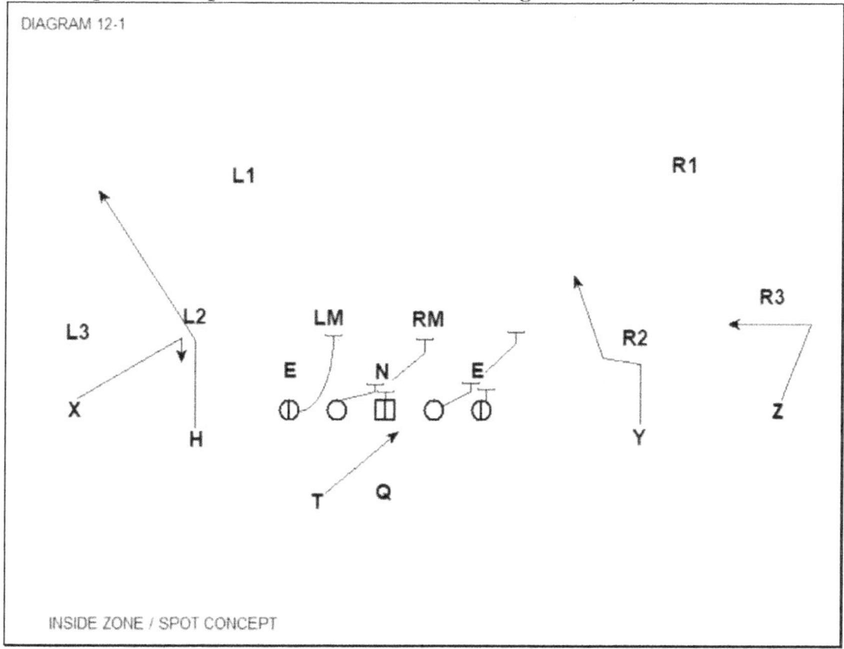

The reason this play is good from 2x2 is because it forces the defense to stay balanced and thereby not be able to bring pressure from as many places without fear of an easy pass play being given up. This RPO has several built-in advantages in that it allows the quarterback two pre-snap Grass Slant Routes to the front door side of the formation. If the quarterback decides to read this play all the way out, then he will mesh with the tailback and read the defensive end. If the end crashed, then the quarterback can execute a triple option post-snap RPO that attacks the L2 defender. If the L2 defender attempts to stop the quarterback, then he will give up and easy throw to the Spot Route. This type of RPO allows the quarterback to have six options spread throughout the play and allows the offense to utilize all eleven players on the offensive side of the ball. The defense is not able to stay gap sound and play all these variations which increases the likelihood that the offense will be able to get the football at least 4th and 2 yards to go to convert.

Another useful RPO is to go back to the ever faithful 3x1 sniffer tight end set and execute a locked inside zone. This play is especially successful versus any sort of six-man box defense. The Now Screen to the outside receiver holds and expands the L1, L2, and L3 away from the box and isolates the Mike Linebacker (Diagram 12-2).

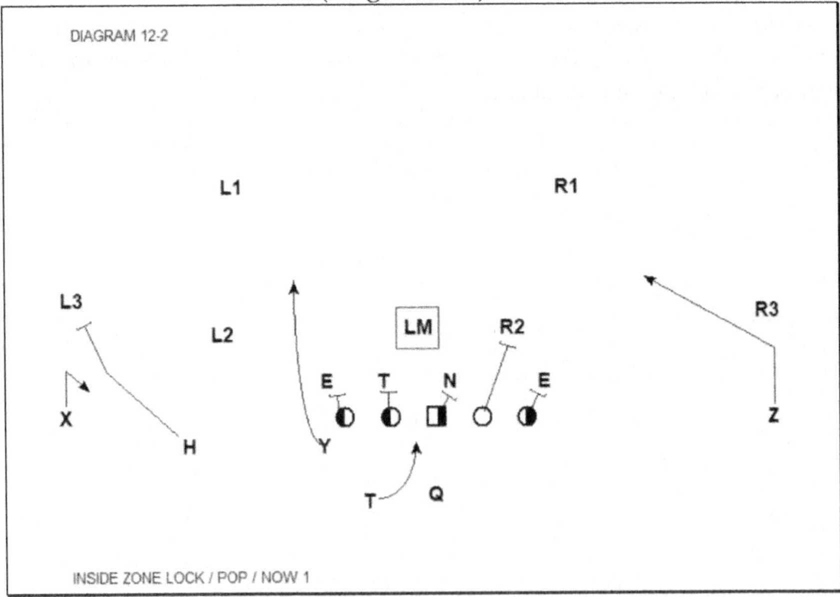

This sort of play gives the quarterback an easy read on the Mike linebacker. If the linebacker plays downhill on the tailback then he is not in position to take away the Pop Pass to the Y receiver. If, however, he feathers to take away the Pop Pass then he is not in position to stop the dive by the tailback and the result should be a positive gain on the run aspect of the play.

A third play that has been useful for us in 2016 and 2017 is a one-word call. A one-word call is defined as a play that is signaled to the defense with just one word from the sideline. The entire offense knows their responsibility based upon this one word. This one-word call is designed to hit the defense quickly say after a gain on 2nd Down and attempt to acquire "cheap" yardage. The unique feature to this play is that the offensive lineman is foot to foot and the tailback executes a Veer Path which is tight into the back-door B gap (Diagram 12-3).

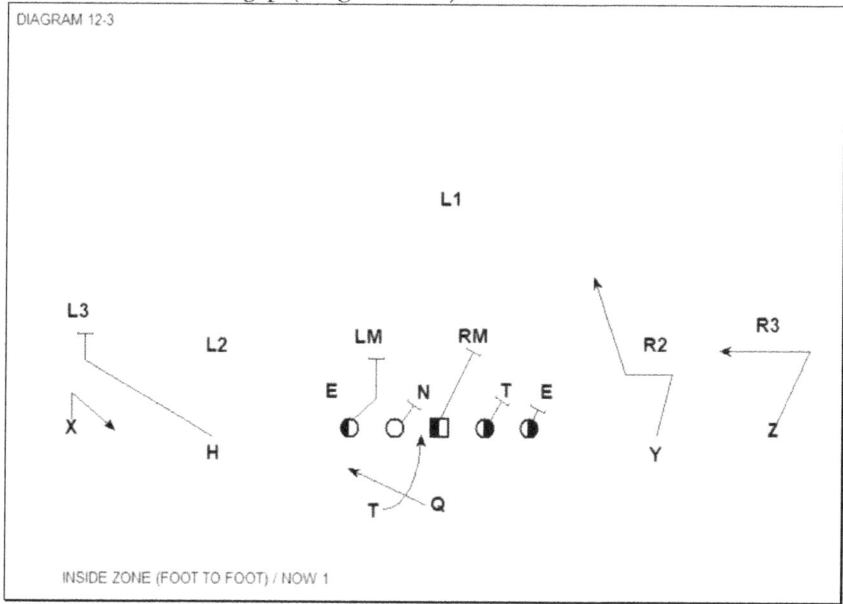

This play has a triple option component out the back door and a pre-snap Grass Concept to the front door like many RPOs in our Surface to Air System arsenal. The unique feature of being foot to foot means that the offensive lineman can essentially wedge forward and gain the running back easy yardage by simply following them. The tight formation means that only the defensive end can stop the diving tailback. If, however, the defensive end stops the tailback the quarterback will have a pull read and will be able to take the triple option RPO into space and create potential havoc on the defensive second and third levels.

Conclusion

Offenses must be able to show a certain measure of success on 3rd Down and Medium. The fact that the offense has arrived at a 3rd Down and Medium is a sign that they have begun to stray at least somewhat from the established philosophy of staying on schedule. This might be because the defense made a good play, a dropped pass, a poor play call, etc. The mission of the play caller is now to get the ball matriculated into a 4th Down and 2 yards to go situation or less so that the head coach can make the determination of whether this is a good situation to risk going for it on 4th Down.

The offense should not be super conservative but also should not take undue risk and feel that they must acquire all the needed real estate all at once. The RPOs that were mentioned above are basically simple and augmented with straightforward reads. It should also catch the reader's eye that there is not a laundry list of plays mentioned but only three for the entire chapter. The reason for this is that a coach should not go looking through a list of plays but should instead have a simple menu of pre-prescribed plays that he has a high level of confidence in for that situation.

As we discussed throughout this work, the quarterback must be coached to understand his role in this drama. He should be coached to make the read and disseminate the ball where it should go and avoid trying to do "too much." When quarterbacks feel they must take undue risk and "be the hero" that is when turnovers and negative plays begin to creep in and it is sometimes best to simply not make a bad situation even worse.

13
3RD & LONG

3rd Down and Long is a situation where the offense faces eight or more yards to attain a 1st Down and a conversion of the chains. This down reflects a generic failure on the part of the offense to maintain methodical positive movement of the football on 1st and 2nd Downs. However, not all is lost.

The offense has two real options at this point which are either to take a shot and attempt to gain the 1st Down all in one play or gain enough yardage to punt the football away. If the chosen method is to imply gain some yardage then there are a host of RPOs that have been and will be categorized in this book that might work. However, this chapter will focus on some of the down the field plays that a coach might utilize to attempt to gain the 1st Down all at once.

It is up to the discretion of the play caller whether this is an opportunity to be aggressive or simply gain some yardage and punt. The location on the field, the time left in the game, the score of the contest are just a few of the factors that might influence a coach to either be aggressive or conservative in a situation such as this.

If it is early in a defensive struggle, then perhaps conservative feelings should take hold whereas the 3rd Quarter of a contest that has seen multiple scores might be a time to take a more aggressive posture. Once again, the quarterback must be coached to understand that just because an aggressive pass play has been called does not mean he has to take that shot down the field. Each of the plays in this category features a check down where the quarterback can go with the ball to gain some yardage and at least let the offense move forward and then safely punt the football away. The Surface to Air System features a Deep to Shallow to Mid read progression.

All the concepts in this chapter feature this read progression.

3rd Down and Long Plays

As we mentioned previously the established goal on 3rd Down and Long is to take a shot and attempt to convert to a 1st Down. However, the offense must have a built-in check down in each of these concepts that allows the quarterback to get the ball out of his hands if the defense drops or brings too many defenders and does not allow him to safely throw the ball down the field. Each of the concepts in this chapter feature some sort of safety check down that is built into the framework of the play. The first such play is a 4 verticals concept paired with a Spot Wheel Concept to the boundary side of the formation (Diagram 13-1).

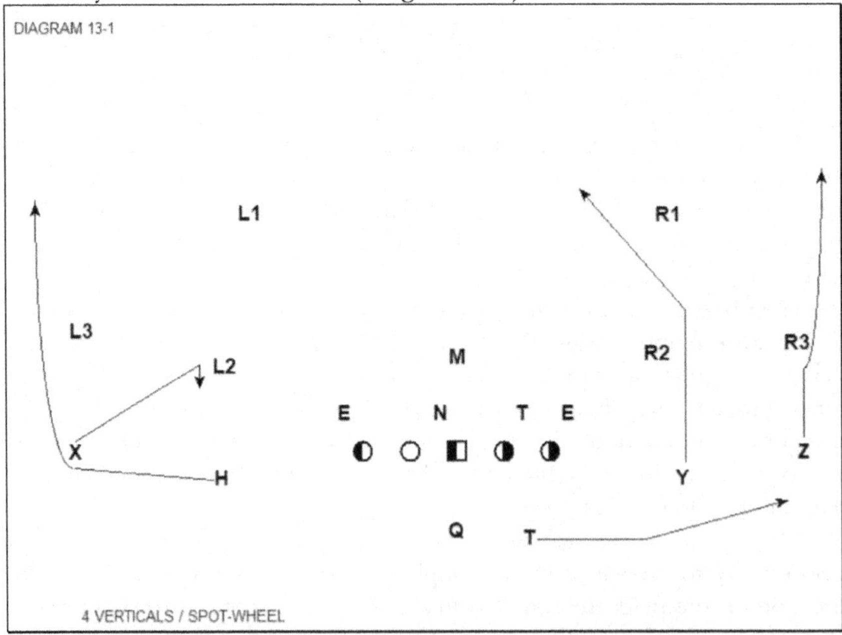

This concept has several intriguing features in that it allows the offense to have three receivers working vertically while two execute man coverage beating routes underneath the vertical receivers. The Spot Concept can convert into a moving crossing route versus man coverage and the Swing Route by the tailback is a natural deterrent to man coverage in that it ties a linebacker to a more athletic athlete in the flats.

This concept also allows the quarterback to have two easy outlet throws should be not be able to hold the football and throw it down the field. The defense is forced to identify the exchanging and manipulating of three different routes on this play in the Seam Bender Route by the Y, the Wheel Route by the H, and the adjusting Spot Route by the X. If the defense plays zone, then there are places to drop the ball off to and gain at least some positive yardage. If, however, the defense elected to roll the dice and play man coverage then they are vulnerable across the field and might give up a 1st Down or even a touchdown.

There are a host of reasons to employ 3x2 sets but one of the best reasons is that is often makes the defense declare their intentions sooner. If the defense intends to bring any pressure versus a 3x2 set, they generally must get their pieces moving a bit sooner than normal. This lack of disguise allows us to call more efficient plays sometimes and get a jump on what the defense is attempting to do pre-snap. A great play to utilize when attempting to do this is the Double Low Option Concept that we have utilized in the Surface to Air System for many years now (Diagram 13-2).

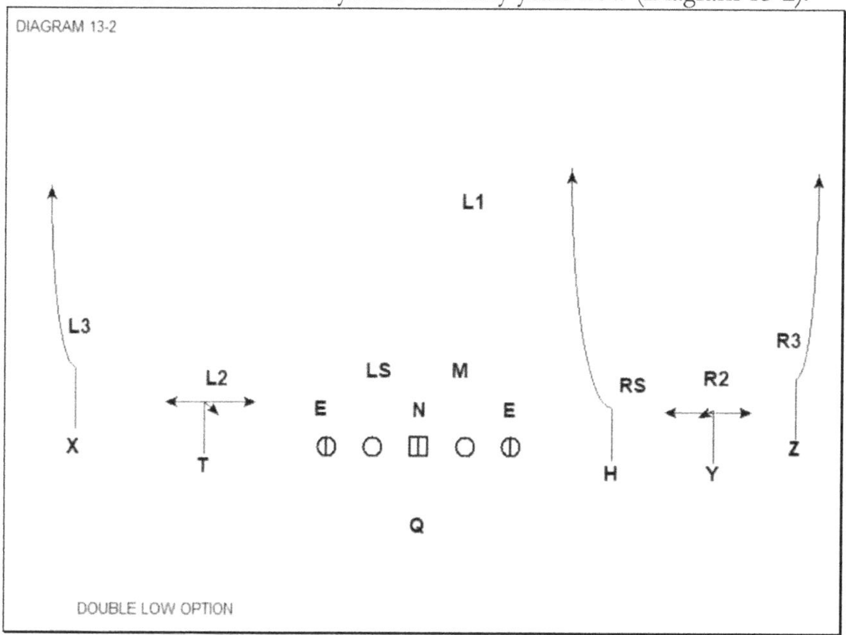

This play features Fade Routes by the outside receivers to give the quarterback an easy pre-snap place to take a shot deep. The tailback executes a Gut Route down the middle of the field in case the defense attempted to roll into a Cover 0 type of coverage and bring pressure. If the defense did this then the matchup of our tailback on one of their linebackers would be a huge advantage for the offense.

The H and Y receivers both execute Low Option Routes which all them to hitch up at 5 steps or bring inside or out away from the leverage of the defender over them. This play has built in components to defeat whatever coverage family the defense decides to employ on this critical down and distance.

A standard answer for many years in the Surface to Air System is to employ some sort of three level Flood Concept into the 3rd Down and Long section of plays. This play is an easy chameleon in the offense in that the play caller can get to it in a variety of ways through route combinations and structures. In 2016 and 2017 one of the most standard ways to do this was through a roll out scheme that employed a Fade Route by the outside receiver, a Bench Route by the second receiver, and a Flat Route by the third receiver (Diagram 13-3).

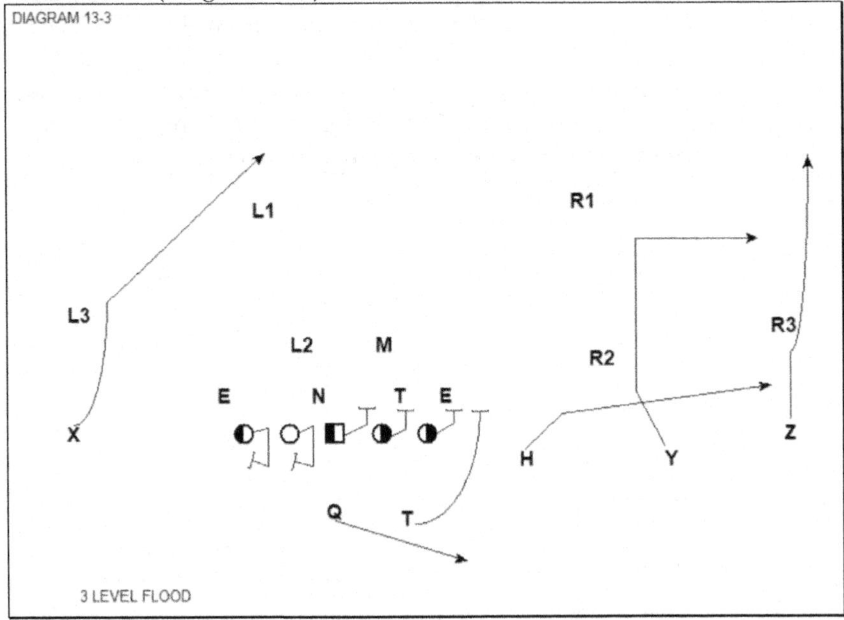

The backside receiver ran a Post Route to hold the safety and give the offense an addition homerun threat to the back side. The quarterback could hold the ball and throw the Fade, Post, or Bench Routes for a big play. This play also features the option for the quarterback to throw to the Flat Route or run the football himself and gain at least a portion of the needed yardage back. The roll out function of the play not only made the quarterback a viable run threat, but it also changed the launch point for the quarterback and allowed him to escape any interior pressure that the defense might have been attempting to utilize.

A fourth commonly utilized play the last few seasons has been the Now 1 Screen Joker play from a 3x1 Flex alignment (Diagram 13-4).

The Flex Formation puts the usually slower Y receiver as the third receiver and moves the more fleet of foot H receiver to the second receiver position. This aids the offense by allowing the faster player to get to the sideline more quickly and allow the normally slower but taller Y receiver to work the Seam Bender route to the inside of the field.

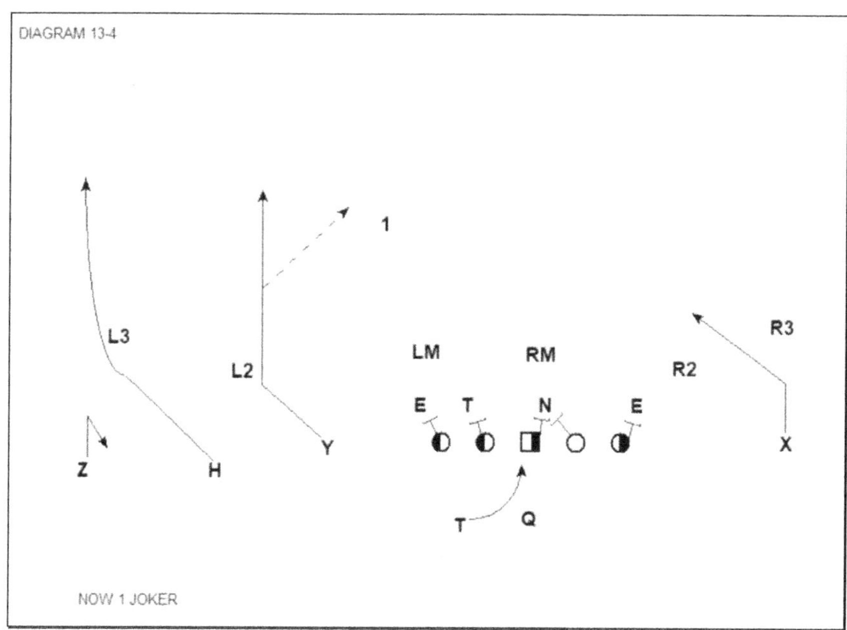

The surface of the play is blocked in pass protection by the offensive lineman and the tailback executes a flash fake to hold the linebackers and provide additional pass protection. The quarterback can take his vertical shot or check the ball down to the Now Screen by the outside receiver should that player be left unguarded when the defense realizes it is a Joker Play and not a screen.

Conclusion

3rd Down and Long is a down where the offensive play caller must decide what the situational structure of the game dictates him to call. If the game is a score fest then perhaps rolling the dice and trying to gain the yardage is worth the risk. If the play caller knows his defense is playing well, he also might take the big shot on this down. This chapter is assuming that the play caller does not elect to utilize a strategy of gain a few yards and punt the ball but instead intends to be aggressive and pursue a 1st Down.

These preceding plays are designed to give the quarterback a few options to take the football down the field and attempt to secure the 1st Down with a single throw. If the quarterback has been coached well, he will also understand that each of these play features a check down component where he can get the ball out of his hands quickly and allow the offense to gain some yardage and put the themselves in a position to perhaps go for it on 4th Down. The offense has always been conditioned by me to understand that if they can hot create a 4th Down and 2 yards to go or less then they should never ask nor assume they will be rewarded with an opportunity to go for the 1st Down on 4th Down.

The offensive personnel are often given the opportunity to correct the "behind the chains" deficiency in one play on 3rd and Long or they can put themselves into a 4th Down and 2 or less category and at least force me to decide. If the quarterback forces a ball and the down becomes 4th and Long, then there is an assumption that we will simply punt the football away and take the ball from his hands. This sort of crystal-clear teaching style makes the quarterbacks decision making not a free-wheeling joy ride but instead a systematic approach to the game of football that lends itself to enhancing his decision making.

14
4TH DOWN

The first big question that must be asked and answered on 4th Down is what is the distance to be gained. The goal is simple; convert to a 1st Down. We do not have any difficult overarching debate about how many yards to achieve here because the goal is simply however many yards, we are from the goal of keeping possession of the ball. If we are going for it on 4th Down, then we obviously want to retain possession and not give it up through a punt.

This chapter will provide two longer yardage types of plays we would call to try and gain the yardage needed, a short yardage play, and a medium distance play. This package is small but so is the sample size of plays in a season where you are going for it on 4th Down for the average team. So once again these should not be a comprehensive list but simply as a taste of what we have done that has been successful for us over the past few seasons in the Surface to Air System.

4th Down Plays

The first two plays in this section are plays that will be called assuming that we must gain a large amount of yardage. Let's make the generic assumption for these two plays that it is 4th Down and 8 yards to go to convert to 1st Down. These first two plays are basically designed to give the quarterback multiple ways to convert that yardage and keep the drive alive. The first play we are going to look at is a concept that we built a few years ago that has been very useful to us called a Ninja Concept (Diagram 14-1).

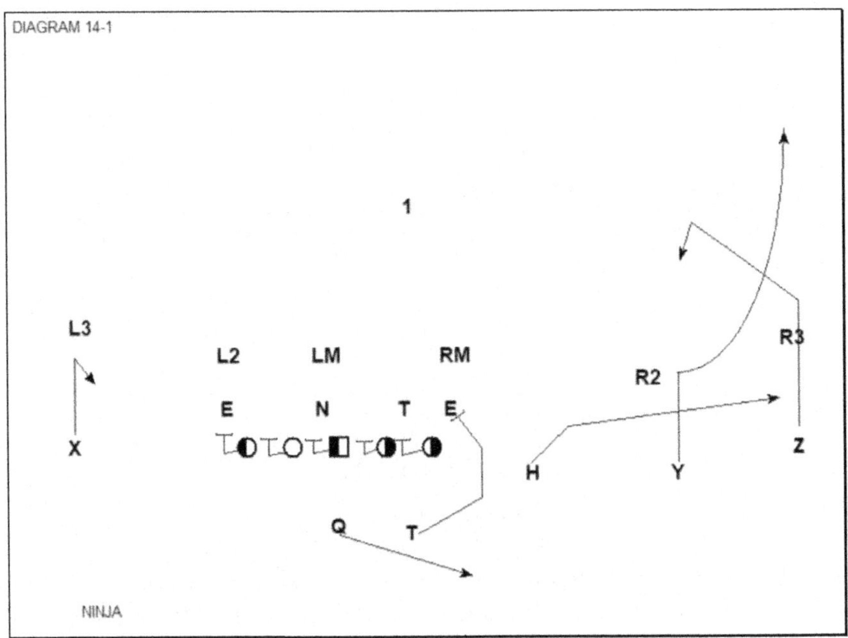

The Ninja Concept starts with the single side receiver being given a Hitch Route as a default setting. The quarterback can throw this Hitch Route or tag it and convert it to a wide variety of other quotes that might allow him to take advantage of a one on one situation and convert the 1st Down very quickly.

If the quarterback cannot play catch with the single side receiver then he will pump fake the ball in that direction and execute a half roll back to the 3x1 side of the formation. The offensive linemen are all sliding to the single side receiver and pass setting to build a wall and the tailback is extending and then reaching c gap defender to the roll out side of the formation. The 3x1 side receivers execute a non-traditional Flood Concept with the outside receiver running a Post-Curl Route, the middle receiver running a Taper Fade Route, and the inside most receiver running a Flat Route.

This play structure then splits the field in half and lets the quarterback either play one on one to the front side or boot around and play with a 3x1 concept that attacks almost all major coverage families including man coverage. This type of play also allows the quarterback the institutional freedom to continue running and pick up the first down with his feet. This play then features four simple pass routes that defeat multiple coverages and a running quarterback. The read progression to the 3x1 side is the Surface to Air System staple of Deep to Shallow to Mid. This is a flexible and highly practical way to help a quarterback to achieve a 1st Down on a 4th and Long-distance call.

Another great way to convert long yardage is to motion the tailback out of the backfield and then bring him on an Under Route beneath a 2x2 4 Verticals Concept (Diagram 14-2).

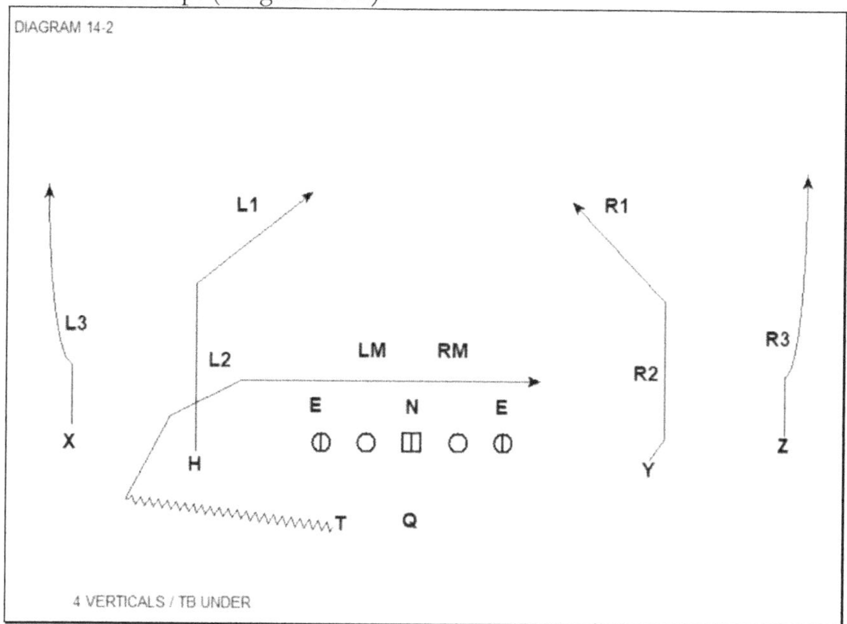

This puts the defense into a balanced set, then unbalances it late, and allows the offense to play in 3x2. All these factors will destroy or distort most pressure schemes but if the defense still blitzes, they will often be at a mismatch against the tailback as he crosses the formation on his route. If, however the defense plays zone then there is a great deal of places to hold the ball and work a throw into versus most standardized zone coverages.

When the offense faces a 4th Down and Short situation, let's say two yards or less to go to convert, then it will need to feature a different set and style of plays.

In this category it is my preference to spread the field and give the quarterback the option to throw, handoff, or run the ball himself. I fell that when he is given this variety of options it increases the likelihood that he will find a hole in the defense just large enough to convert those badly needed two yards. One highly successful way to do this is to employ a 2x2 Stack formation and execute an inside zone with Double Bubble Screen concept from it (Diagram 14-3).

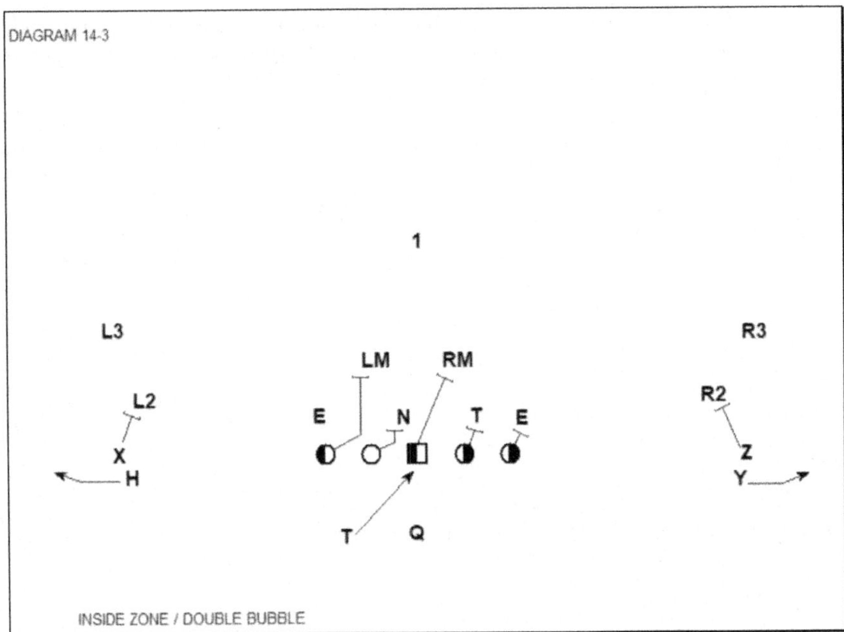

The stacked receivers are lined up so wide from the offensive lineman that it forces the defense to extend themselves away from the box further than they are comfortable doing. If the defenders do not remove with the stack it is our philosophy to tell the quarterback to throw that ball even if it is 4th Down and 2. We have a philosophy and philosophies don't atrophy, they don't shrink, and they certainly don't get shelved when the money is on the table.

Quite the contrary, we have a philosophy of forcing the defense to cover us down and if they don't cover us down then we throw the football and this concept holds true wherever and whenever we find it to be the case. If the defense does remove four defenders from the box and play with at least one high safety, then the quarterback can play zone read football and control the defensive end with his read and play with a numbers advantage in the box. This is the sort of simple, yet ingenious, type of play calling that we like to utilize on 4th Down and Short and is a style that has served us well over the last few seasons.

The final 4th Down category that we should elaborate on then is the 4th Down and Medium category. This situation would be considered let's say 4th Down and 5 yards to go for a conversion. In this instance I have always liked to block the front solid with the offensive lineman and throw double quick game to each side of the field. One of our better options in this category has been to execute a Snag Concept to one side of the field with the Slant Option Concept to the other, usually boundary, side of the field (Diagram 14-4).

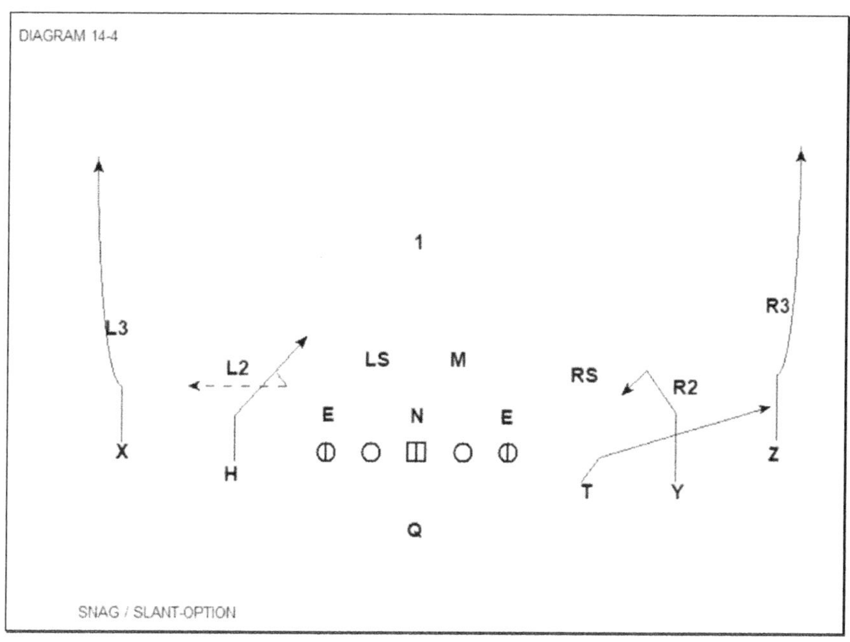

The reason this play has been so useful is that the Snag Concept beats most commonly called zone coverages while the Slant Option Concept is devastatingly successful against man coverage teams. With concepts that complement each other so well and defeat multiple coverage families this type of play is a great opportunity to get the ball into athletic player's hands very quickly.

There is minimal risk here is taking a sack, and unless the quarterback makes an egregious mistake, very little chance of an interception. This call creates great run after the catch potential also which might make a four yard throw a fourteen-yard gain and create explosive play opportunities against risk taking defenses.

Conclusion

4th Down is the technical definition of the money down. The offense and the defense are both aware that they must make a play here or the game will be fundamentally altered in one or the other's favor very quickly. If the defense makes a big stop, they will have the ball and momentum for their offense.

If, however, the offense makes a big play they will have a fresh set of downs to play with and a defense that is demoralized and back on its heels. These are the sorts of downs that are a game inside the game. These plays can help make or break a game and define where the momentum of the game is headed. The distance that is needed in order to convert so obviously a major consideration and has been discussed above. It is important that a play caller have a host of answers for 4th Down because it is so important. However, a useful piece of advice is to remember that even though the offense should have answers and some of that might need some window dressing to make them look unique, the offense should try and stay as much inside their lane as possible.

Whole new plays with too many gadgets can make the offensive players lose confidence in the base scheme. Now, having said that the mantra of "we do what we do" is sometimes not enough on these types of plays. That balance of new twists and tried and true strategies must be balanced and utilized on this most critical of downs for the offense to flourish throughout the season.

15
COMING OUT

Throughout this book we have focused on the down and distance portion of calling plays. We will now transition to a more field-oriented view of calls plays. We will start to look at how we in the Surface to Air System call plays based upon where we are located on the field. The first section we want to consider is a portion of the field that we identify as the coming out yardage area.

This yardage area for us is anytime the ball is spotted inside our own ten-yard line. If we receive a kickoff or a punt or force a turnover and we get the ball outside the coming out area, then we have a different philosophical view of what to accomplish. When the ball is acquired inside the ten-yard line a special consideration is in play. The problem that we have in this area is that we are in the shadow of our own goal line and we do not have enough room to safely punt the ball past midfield. Therefore, our goal in this area must to be to achieve at least one 1st Down.

The previous chapter's discussion of downs and distances should be maintained and utilized even though the ball is backed up here. However, there is special consideration about what plays to call simply because we are so close to our own goal line. The plays we call here are sometimes not divergent from the previous down and distance calls that we utilized throughout this book, but sometimes we feel that we need to alter this strategy a bit. In this chapter we will discuss and analyze three plays that we have found over the past few years that increase the likelihood that we can achieve a 1st Down.

These plays are all designed to create a high probability of getting four yards or more on each play. We would love to score a touchdown from this area of the field, but we are also realistic enough to know that the defense has a great deal of leverage on us in this area of the field. The defense can bring a variety of pressure schemes here and feel certain that disaster won't strike because they have so much field left to give. Our goal then is to play the game one 1st Down at a time when backed up here. If we can achieve one 1st Down, then we feel that we at least will not have to punt from our end zone and we create the possibility at a minimum of being able to punt the ball onto the other side of the 50-yard line. The following plays are not designed to score but to simply acquire four yards and allow us to accomplish our goal. There are times we choose not to be so conservative in this area of the field but by and large we boil our goals down to a simple destination of just ten yards in front us.

Coming Out Plays

These coming out plays need to be very simple and have a high probability of success. One of the things we like is to play from a 3x2 set down here, especially if we are inside the five-yard line and are likely to be snapping the ball to our quarterback near or inside our own end zone. When the quarterback must mesh with the tailback it is another opportunity for ball exchange issues and some young players get nervous doing this inside their own end zone.

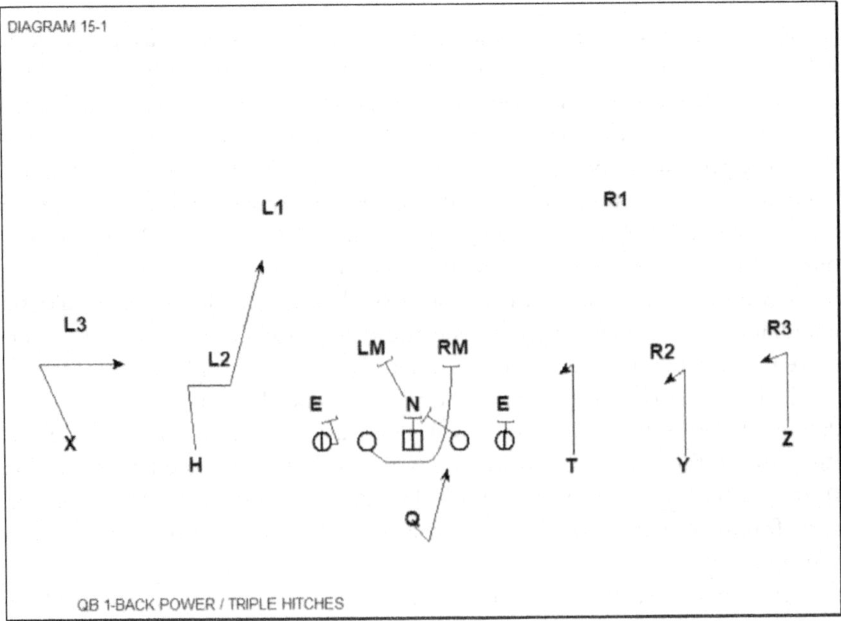

Therefore, it is our preference to get into 3x2 RPOs in this area that alleviate the need for a mesh point between the quarterback and the tailback. This also lessons the number of things for the quarterback to process and makes the game a handoff or a pass play simple proposition for him. The first such play is to put the offense into a 3x2 set and run the 1 Back Power Play at a three receiver Hitch Route surface (Diagram 15-1).

This simple RPO allows the quarterback to throw the Grass Concept as his pre-snap look or to read the play all the way out and throw the Hitch Routes if the defense collapses on him while running the power play. This sort of simplistic yet effective RPO keeps the quarterback from having to read defenders while meshing inside his own end zone.

Another high-quality RPO, as you move out of the shadow of your own end zone, is to run inside zone with Double Slant Option Concepts from a 2x2 set (Diagram 15-2).

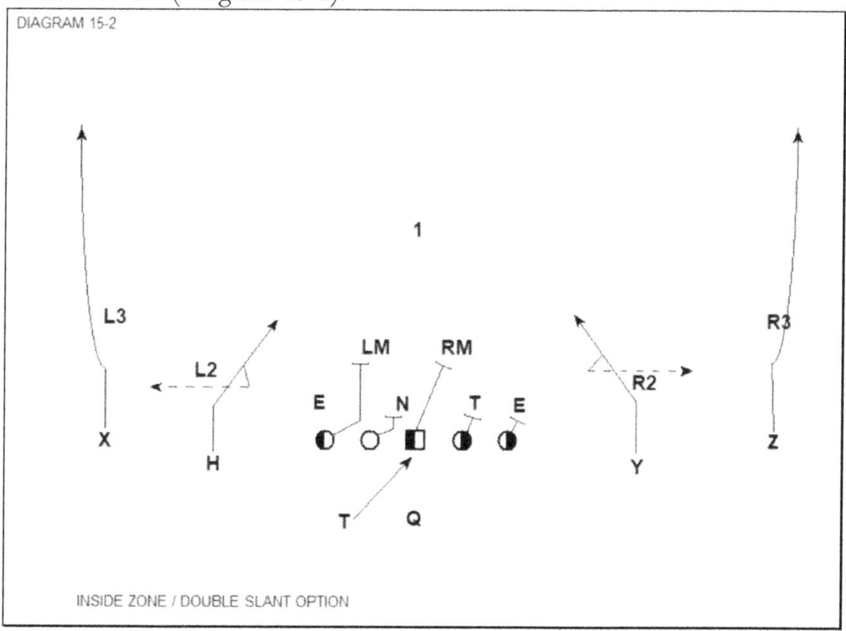

The inside zone is simple and highly executed by the offensive lineman and the defensive end is eliminated by the quarterback's read. The Double Slant Option Concepts that are mirrored here give both the Y and H receivers a two way go to win versus the L2 and R2 defenders.

If the defense does not do an adequate job of taking away inside pressure, then the Slant Routes will provide an easy throw for the quarterback. If, however, the defense elects to compress these routes or play man coverage here the offense has easily convertible routes that can get outside and gain significant yardage. This sort of play keeps the game small and simple for the quarterback and allows him to play fast with a variety of options at his disposal.

A third variable option for the offense to utilize is the ubiquitous sniffer 3x1 set that is seen becoming more and more common throughout the high school and college ranks today. This set has the advantage of allowing the play caller to have three receivers to one side of the formation, a tight end or 11 personnel grouping, and a variety of surface changing propositions using that sniffer.

The advantages of playing with a sniffer tight end are myriad but one of my personal favorites is the opportunity to load option the defense. The Surface to Air System refers to a load block as the sniffer tight end going around the defensive end, who is being read by the quarterback, and blocking the linebacker that rests behind the read defensive end. Many defenses will employ a squeeze/scrape technique where they will crash the defensive end and scrape the linebacker around to hit the quarterback after he pulls the football to run.

This is a defensive countermeasure to the proliferation of RPO based offenses in the game today. However, a load option by the offense with a Spot Concept to the outside of it effectively eliminates this defensive countermeasure (Diagram 15-3).

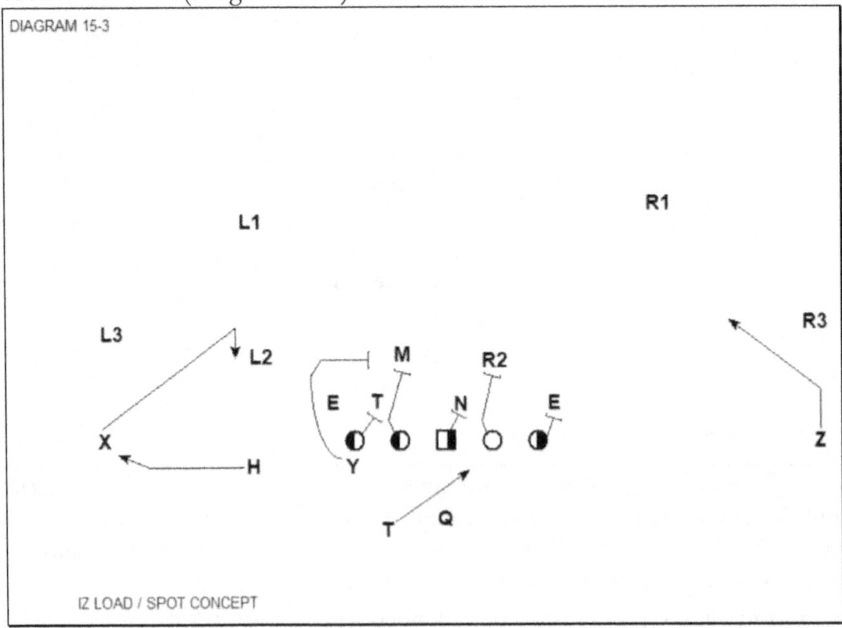

The quarterback can throw the Spot Concept or Grass Concept as a pre-snap read or he can read the defensive end for the give or pull of the football. If the defense plays squeeze/scrape their defensive end will take the tailback but their linebacker will be prevented from scraping to the quarterback by the load block of the sniffer tight end. This will allow the quarterback to penetrate the second level of the defense and then read the L2 player and place him in conflict between the quarterback run and the

Spot Concept. This is a highly effective way to use the quarterback's running ability and create a higher level of stress for the defense.

Conclusion

The coming out situation can be a stressful one for the offense if they get behind the chains early. It is for that reason that the Surface to Air System employs a series of easy to read and easy to execute RPOs that allow us to make a 1st Down and get the ball away from our own goal line. If the offense is successful, then it can get into its natural play calling groove and move forward.

If the offense is not able to make a 1st Down, then it should have at least managed to gain a few yards and at least give the punter some needed room to get off a punt that can be safely covered. For us, this is not a time to take massive risks, although at times we have done so, it is instead a time to play the law of averages and attempt to get the ball out of harm's way where the offense can operate more effectively. It has been my experience that offensive players are very hesitant around their own end zone and so removing the offense from this area tends to increase the offensive player's confidence level and degree of efficiency.

16
OUR OWN 10 TO THE 25

Once the ball has been advanced past our own ten-yard line the goal of the offense now changes. We are presumed to be in space between our own ten- and twenty-five-yard lines for the purpose of this chapter. In this space of the field we are focusing on flipping the field. The definition of flipping the field is making sure that the offense can end their possession, through a punt or loss of possession on downs, inside the opponents thirty-yard line.

In order to accomplish this goal, the offense must be able to string together a series of 1st Down conversions. If the offense takes control of the ball at its own twenty-five-yard line, then it is presumed the offense must get at least two 1st Downs before it can put the ball away and be assured that the field has been flipped.

It should be noted that the offense is still attempting to score and is still attempting to make big plays but the overall philosophy here is to simply make sure the field is flipped. This may sound like a weird goal, but it is rooted in the reality of how football games unfold. A seasoned play caller knows that the more often the ball is played on the opponent's side of the field the greater the likelihood that he will have the opportunity to score points on the opposing defenses.

If the ball is first marched onto the opposing team's side of the field or punted there the opposing offense must be proficient in order to get it back across mid-field. If the opposition cannot do this then the offense will start getting short fields and increased opportunities to score points. This strategy can falter if the score gets out of control and the time becomes short. There are certainly times when an offense will have to push the envelope in this area of the field, but we are assuming this is a close or tied game for the purpose of this study.

We will continue to call many RPOs between the ten- and twenty-five-yard lines. These PROs will take on an increasingly aggressive and more complicated nature as the offense progresses further from its own goal line. The RPOs that we will employ will begin to attack further down the field and add more motions and formations tweaks in order to get more yards more quickly.

Our Own 10 to 25 Yard Line Plays

While the majority of RPOs in this section have more window dressing on them but some are still quite simple. A play that have been a staple for us for six seasons now is a play that we have title "Empty Wave." The Empty or 3x2 Wave Play is a one-word RPO that is designed to attack the entire width of the football field simultaneously (Diagram 16-1).

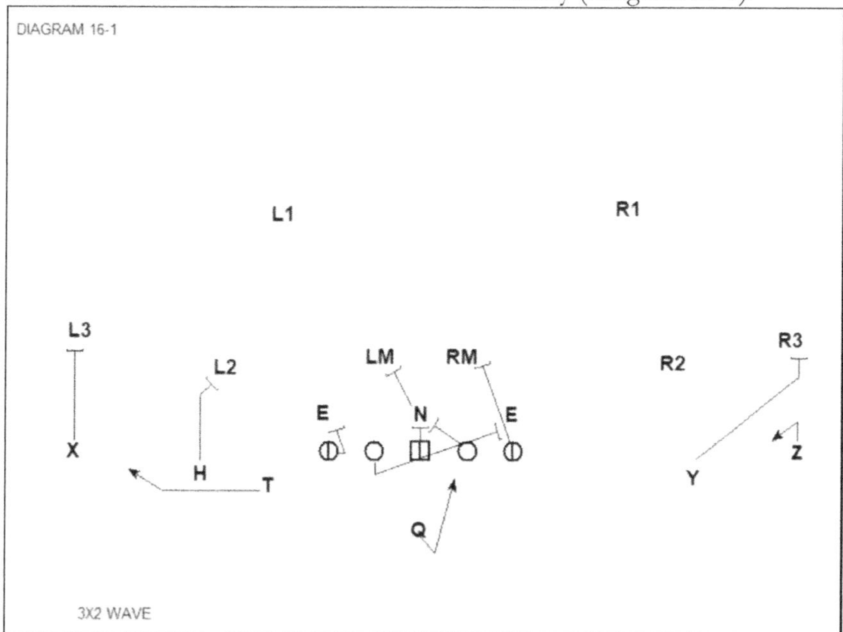

The two receivers on the right side of the formation execute a Now 1 Screen while the three receivers on the left side of the formation execute a Bubble Screen to the #3 receiver. This double Now Screen structure is complimented with some sort of interior run between the tackles. The run play that is utilized can vary from week to week and opponent to opponent.

The reason it must be an interior run is that we want to stress and expand the defense in three equal sections and so the run play must stay up the middle of the field. In this case we are utilizing a Long Trap Concept because it creates superior blocking angles versus an odd front defense. While inside zone can be a good concept for Wave it is usually best to utilize a gap, scheme run for the purpose of angle creation. This play places a maximum amount of stress on the defense and forces them to defend all the width of the football field simultaneously.

Placing the offense in a 3x1 set and then locking the inside zone is a great way to also conflict odd man front defenses (Diagram 16-2).

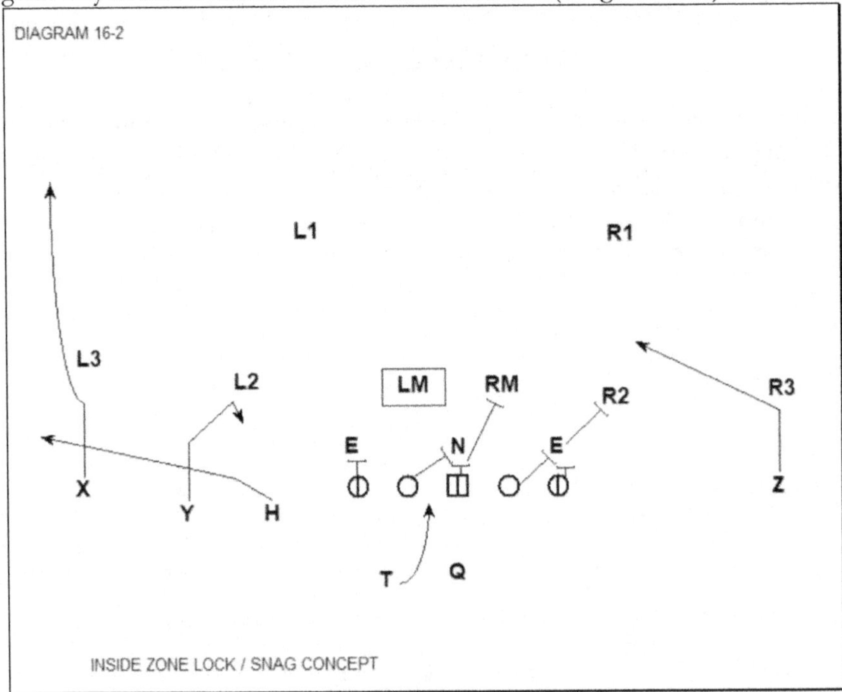

The Left Mike is forced to determine if he will match numbers and give the defense three defenders in the flat to match the offense's Snag Concept or if he will remain in the box. The quarterback is easily able to read this action and throw to the Snag Concept or hand the ball into the box based upon what reaction he sees post-snap. If the defense attempts to bring the extra defender from the other side of the field, a tactic we call "Cowboying Over", then the quarterback will throw the single wide receiver route and attack the void area in the defense.

With the goal of flipping the field it helps for the offense to introduce more window dressing on the defense in the form of formational variations and motions. It is essential that the offense not allow the defense to establish a routine and get comfortable with how the offensive structure appears to them each play. To accomplish this window dressing the offense must be willing to change the surface. Changing the surface refers to the offense's willingness to make basic plays look different to the defense either through a pre-snap formational change or motion that inherently changes the way the defense sees the offense's structure. One way to accomplish this is to line up in a 2x2 sniffer set to the left and orbit motion the H receiver into a pass play relationship outside the sniffer (Diagram 16-3).

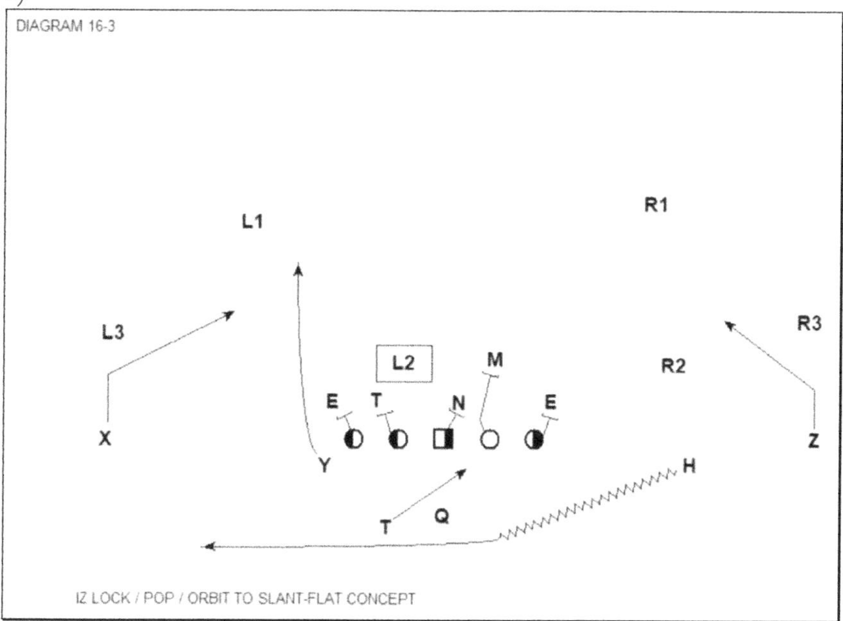

This play features a locked inside zone call with a POP Pass by the sniffer and a Slant Flat Concept by the X receiver and the motioning H receiver. This sort of surface change is devastating to the defense because they can't simply bump defenders over with the sniffer running a Seam POP Pass. This play distorts and potentially destroys the basic structure of the defense and gives the offense the ability to move from a 2x2 to a 3x1 set. This orbit motion has been useful in changing the surface for many years but when paired with the sniffer tight end, it creates a substantive difference for the defense to process.

A great formation for us has always been a 2x2 Split Set that features three wide receivers and two running backs flanking the quarterback. In recent years we have expanded upon this formation and added a 3x1 Split Set that calls for the tailback and H receiver to line up on the same side of the formation next to one another. This formation can be coupled with a sniffer tight end that makes it more devastating for the defense to process and a formation that can lead to bigger gains. The offense can now call and inside zone with a sniffer insertion and allow the H receiver to swing to the flat (Diagram 16-4).

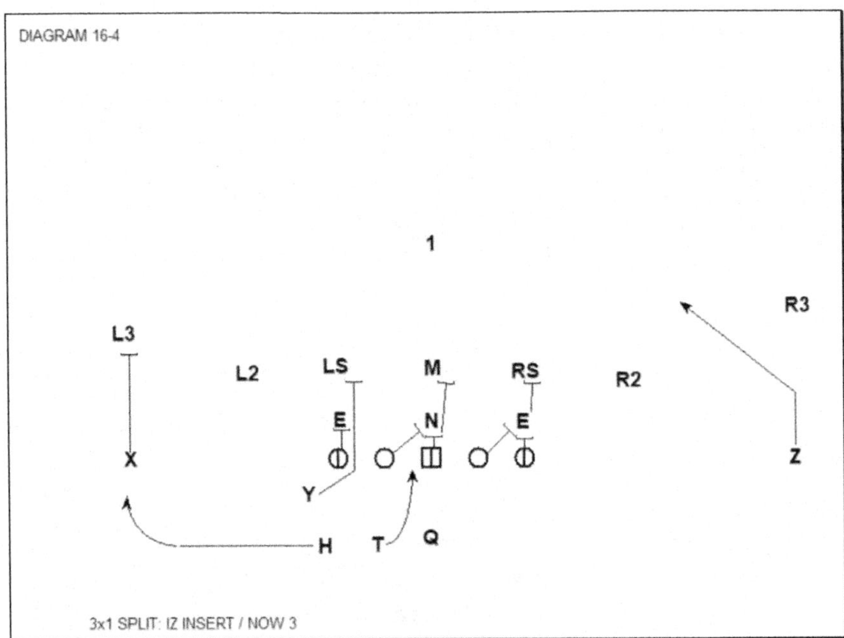

This play allows the offense to cancel out the L3 and L2 players and block the Left Stack Linebacker in a 3-3 defense. The defense is essentially disallowed from bringing any extra defenders in the box and is almost forced to allow the offense to run an isolation play.

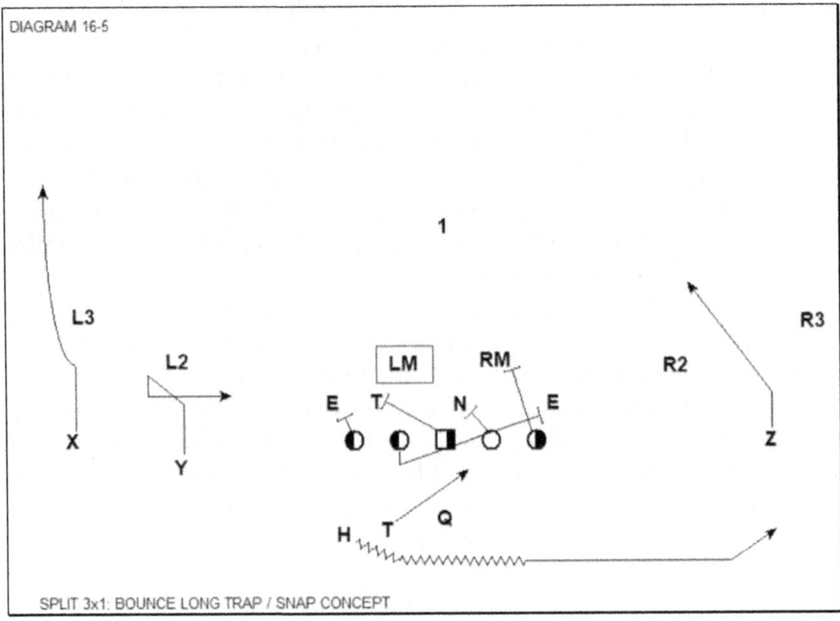

If the defense is constructed in a way that the play caller wants to keep them balanced and use this formation, then he can bounce motion the H receiver back to the front door side. This motion will force the defense from an unbalanced defense back into a balanced set and allow the play caller to tag any sort of two man pass concept he prefers onto the back-door side of the play (Diagram 16-5).

The play caller can attach any sort of interior run, a gap scheme usually offers great angles for the offensive lineman in this case, and then have a balanced look where he can allow the quarterback to read both the L2 and the R2 defenders. If either the L2 or R2 attempt to play inside the box, then the quarterback will throw off their movement. However, if the defense stays balanced and equals numbers on the printer then the quarterback can hand the ball into the box and play the numbers advantage there.

The Snap Concept that the quarterback has available to him to the back-door side here will defeat the L2 and come late back into the Left Mike's area of responsibility. If the Left Mike plays heavy on the run the quarterback has an opportunity to throw a post-snap read off that movement.

Conclusion

The goal of the offense when the ball is located between our ten and our twenty-five-yard line is to flip the field. Flipping the field to us is defined as placing the ball at the end of our possession at least on our opponents thirty-yard line. This accomplishes a few goals. First, this prevents our defense from a facing a short field and a situation where the offense can call plays aggressively with the goal of scoring. Second, it allows our defense to play aggressive when they take the field versus the opposing offense. Finally, it increases the likelihood that we will regain possession of the ball in a place on the field favorable to us starting and finishing a drive that results in points.

The plays that we call in this area need to start to depart from our and the defense's comfort zones. We need to start adding formations, motions, and route tags that complicate the defense's abilities to process our offense quickly and efficiently. We, as a system of offense, must start to open the game up and "do more" as we are entering this portion of the field. It should be noted, however, that we are not departing from our base philosophy of down and distance nor are we going to take undue risks here. What we are going to do is change the surface and begin to add window dressing to our plays to gain more yardage and get more 1st Downs to get to the fifty-yard line where our next chapter will pick up and expound upon our Surface to Air System philosophy.

17
OUR OWN 25 TO THE 50

There is a seismic shift in play calling once an offense successfully reaches the fifty-yard line. In order to get there the offense must gain some large chunks of yardage. In high school football there is a generic struggle on the part of offenses to matriculate the ball down the field without the aid of big plays. A big play for us is defined as any play that gains ten or more yards.

The goal of the Surface to Air System is to create 1st Downs and score touchdowns. In order to accomplish this goal, the offense must be able to move the ball down the field. The defense is aware that if they can force the offense to snap the ball many times, then eventually the offense will make some sort of mistake. An athlete will hold, drop a pass, jump off sides, or some other infraction that will take the offense off schedule and create a lessened opportunity to score points. In order to prevent this the offense must switch over and become more aggressive at some point. The offense must get bigger chunks of yardage and not be forced to earn every single 1st Down all the way down the field. The offense must be able to get large chunks of yardage and thereby get into scoring position before it makes some mistake that shifts the balance of power back to the defense.

The offense would have to earn two and a half 1st Downs from the twenty-five-yard line to reach midfield. This is a long distance and many plays especially for a high school offense, to be sound and not make a single mistake. If the offense can achieve say a twenty-two-yard gain while on their own twenty-five-yard line, then they would only need one more play and three more yards to gain midfield. If the offense needed three downs to get a 1st Down, then they would need closer to eight plays to travel the same distance matriculating the ball. Therefore, the plays called in this section of the field begin to open the aggressive tendencies of the offense up more.

There is a greater emphasis on bigger chunks of yardage and the quarterback is encouraged to throw these RPOs a bit further down the field. The offense is no longer principally concerned with getting out of its own end zone or flipping the field but instead wants to pick up as much real estate in as few plays as possible. This chunking of the field from the twenty-five to fifty-yard lines is not an accident and is not something that will happen without specific intervention by the play caller.

The plays called in this section will be a bit riskier but still involve the same simple and basic reads that have always been a hallmark of the system. The quarterback is still encouraged to consider down and distance and still put the offense in the best situation to make 1st Downs, However, the aggressiveness is slightly more elevated and the quarterback should be encouraged to "go for it" a bit more when deciding whether or not to push the ball further down the field on these plays.

Our 25 to the 50 Yard Line Plays

We are in a big chunk acquisition mode once we have attained our own twenty-five-yard line. The closer the ball gets to midfield the larger chunks of yardage we want our quarterback to attempt to acquire. The offense wants to run certain plays from certain sets and one of our best sets is a 3x1 sniffer set with outside zone executed to the field.

This play is a staple of the Surface to Air System because it attacks the width of the field and forces the defense to play honestly against some of the other things we are attempting to do offensively. The defense can utilize a variety of countermeasures to this set, but their most common answer is to roll late from a two high safety look into a one high safety look to get an extra defender into the box. The offense can call an RPO featuring the single side receiver on a five step Glance Post Route to attack the grass where that safety would be rotating out of on the back-door side of the play (Diagram 17-1).

If the safety rolls to the middle of the field so that the front door safety can add his hat to the run fit, then the defense is vulnerable to this Post Route and can potentially give up a large chunk of yardage. This is the type of play that is slightly higher risk and higher reward that the offense can start to utilize. If the quarterback reads the defenses' s intention correctly then he either hands the ball to the tailback for a decent gain to the wide side of the field or he throws a Post Route to the boundary, either way the offense is likely to acquire a big chunk of much needed real estate.

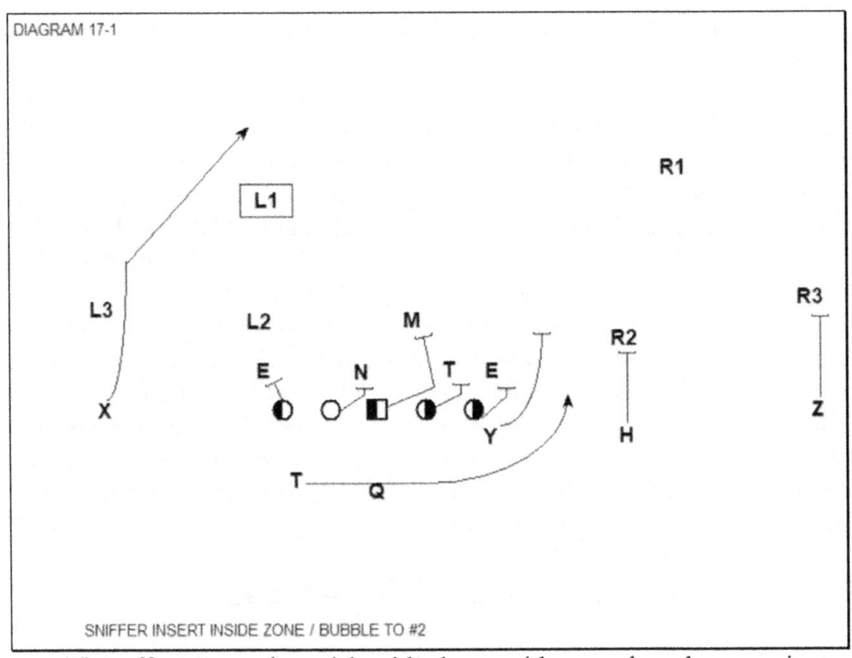

The offense can also stick with the outside zone-based run against a one high defense like the 3-3 stack. The defense must decide how they will process the back door 3x1 side of the formation as the offense runs wide to the single side of the formation. The offense can then feature a man coverage or one high beating RPO that we dubbed a Spear Concept (Diagram 17-2).

The Spread Concept is just the RPOs modern adaptation of the old West Coach Texas Concept. This play features an inside receiver holding a defender down with a Hitch Route while a Post Route is being executed behind that route. The defense can quickly match the Hitch Route and take it away but if they do so they are vulnerable to the Glance Post Route breaking open behind them. Of course, the defense could push a linebacker and the free safety both to the 3x1 side off the formation and stop this pass play, but they would likely give up a big chunk of yardage then to the outside zone running tailback to the single side receiver of the formation.

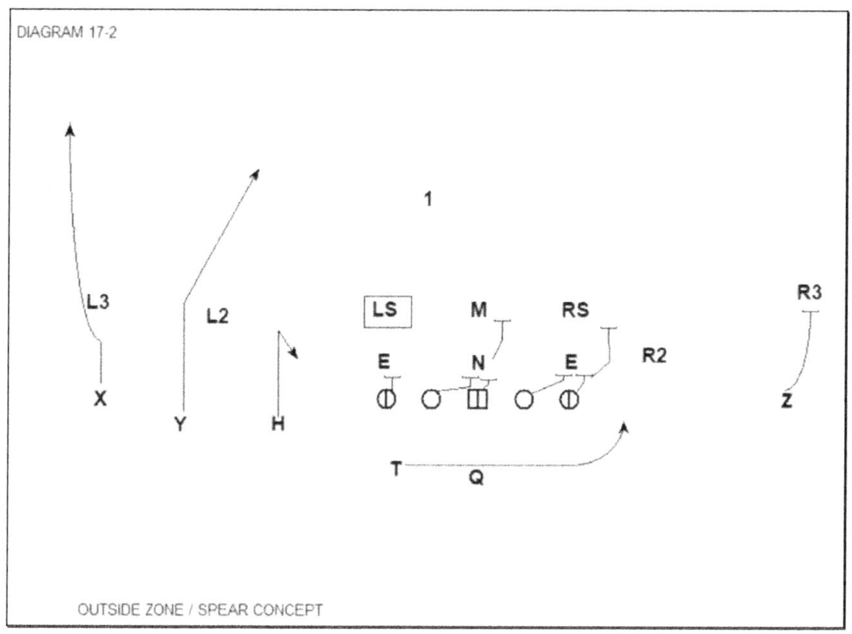

Another great way to get to the Post Route is using a concept that the Surface to Air System calls a Squirrel Concept (Diagram 17-3).

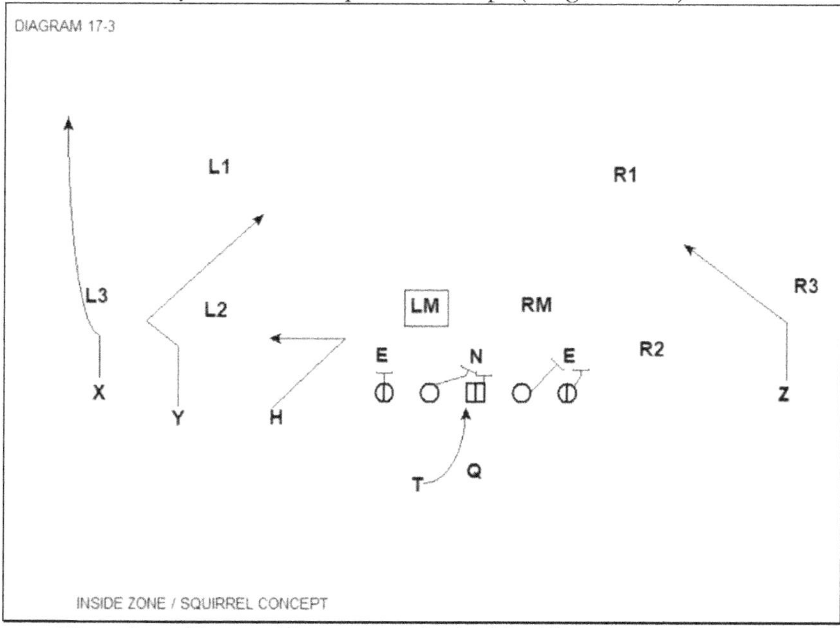

Now the offense will execute a locked inside zone and read the Left Mike to determine if the will play the box or play the 3x1 receiver structure.

The two double move routes executed by the Y and H receivers will cause both the second and the third levels of the defense to become distorted and potentially displaced. This sort of RPO could be run anywhere on the field but as it offers the quarterback the chance to hold the ball longer and attack more into the third level of the defense, it is a perfect complement to our philosophy of attempting to acquire chunks of yardage.

The preceding RPOs all allow the offense to attack into the second and the third levels of the defense regardless of whether they play from a one or two high safety structure. These plays are more aggressive in nature and cause the quarterback to hold the ball slightly longer and hopefully acquire larger chunks of yardage.

The play caller may elect to stay with the RPO world throughout this section, but we commonly like to jump outside that world for a few plays once we get into this section of the field. A great way to do this is to block the surface of the defense solid and throw mirrored quick game pass concepts. One of the preferred ways to do this is to get into a 3x2 structure and throw Double Taper Fade Concepts and add into that play a tailback Gut Route (Diagram 17-4).

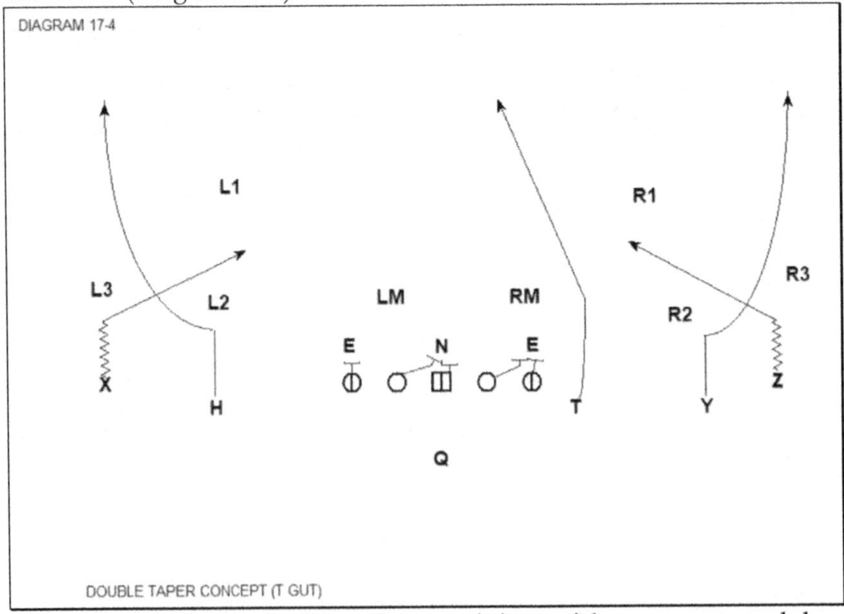

This play is a good call here because it is a quick game route and does not require the quarterback to execute a long drop and risk a sack but still attacks the back half of the secondary. This play also has the advantage that it attacks both a one high structure and a two high safety structure. Finally, should the defense elect to play man coverage then the outside receivers have a rub and an opportunity to get open and the tailback on a linebacker is likely a mismatch in favor of the offense. This play called was used extensively in 2016 and 2017 in this area of the field and became a quality answer to gaining large chunks of yardage between the twenty-five- and fifty-yard lines.

Conclusion

Acquiring chunks of yardage on play calling should not be a risky affair but instead one that just requires a degree of creativity. The offense is attempting to avoid a situation where the defense can force them into a protracted struggle for yardage and thereby buy time and await an offensive penalty or turnover. Many defenses today will trade yards for time in the hopes that the offense will make a mistake and take themselves out of favorable down and distance structures.

This means it is particularly necessary for the offense to make larger chunks of yardage between the twenty-five- and fifty-yard lines. These plays do not need to be, and are often not, high risk/high reward drop back passes that involve the quarterback holding the ball and receivers executing complicated routes. Instead these are many of the same general plays the offense has already featured with slightly more emphasis on reading the second and third levels of the defense and pushing the ball slightly further down the field.

A slight variation in route structure and the use of a few more double moves in this area of the field add to the possibility of larger gains of yardage. If the offense can be successful gaining some larger chunks of yardage and getting inside the fifty-yard line quickly then they increase their opportunity to get to the red zone faster and score more points. If a defense is conservative in this area, then the offense should get some chunk plays. If the defense is aggressive in this area, then the offense might get some chunk plays and even get to the red zone or end zone ahead of schedule.

18
THE 50 YARD LINE TO THE OPPONENT'S 10

In each of the chapters of this work we have looked at the core Surface to Air System philosophy that surrounds the basis of the down and distance or field position. At no point in this work have we yet said that the goal is to score. That all changes with this chapter. Our goal, once we cross the fifty-yard line is very simple, our goal is to score.

We don't think of scores in the sense of a field goal. We want to score a touchdown once we cross the fifty-yard line. We are planning for the offense to go for it on 4th Down once we begin to really penetrate this area and we are much more aggressive in our play calling. In this portion of the field we anticipate that the defense might also realize we have more downs and more options at our disposal to score points.

We anticipate that the defense may elect to be more aggressive in using their pressure schemes and perhaps playing many coverages with it. The defense knows that we will take more shots here and so they will often run to the poles, which means they will play one extreme style of defense or the other. We see teams that drop eight defenders into coverage and play for the aggressive pass and we see teams that match up and play Cover 1 or Cover 0 to force the issue. In either case, we must be ready to take advantage of whatever the defense is doing, and we must call plays that have a more "devil may care" attitude to them. This is not an area of the field where we are timid, for here we wish to get points on the board.

We will still utilize RPOs in this section, as we will chronicle in the next few pages, but we also take greater risks by throwing the ball down the field. In this section we will also use more of our QSO package and our PAP Series. These plays allow us to combat the defense if the drop to the extreme of flooding zones, but they also give us great answers should the defense elect to roll the dice and play more aggressive with man coverage and bring pressure. The play calling strategies we discussed based upon down and distance earlier still bears witness, especially when the offense first crosses the fifty-yard line.

As the offense begins to move the ball and gain more yardage, there is a point where there is no longer a serious consideration of punting the football. This realization means that the play caller can essentially play with two 1st and 10 calls and be more aggressive in pushing the envelope as the play caller knows that he is essentially in four down territory for most of this section of the field.

50 Yard Line to the 10 Yard Line Plays

It is essential that the offense feature plays in this area of the field that gives it a high probability of scoring touchdowns. I used to think this section of the field was all about plays. As time has gone on and I have become a more experienced play caller, I have come to realize that it matters much more that you get the ball to your players more than you worry about the plays you call.

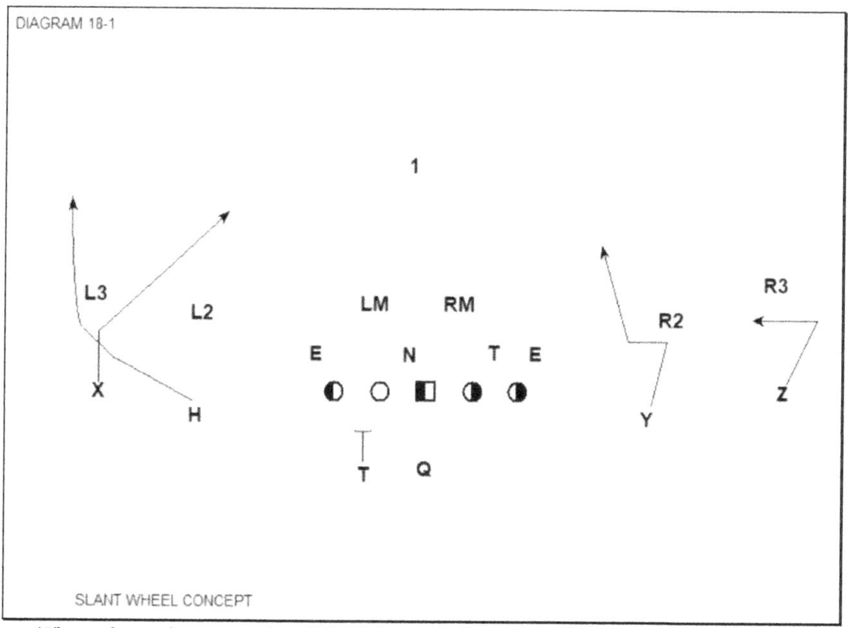

SLANT WHEEL CONCEPT

The adage that you should "think of players and not plays" is very much true in this part of the field. A good play caller should begin to think about who his ball players are and what sorts of plays get the ball in their hands quickly and allow them to make big plays in this area of the field. Of course, getting the ball to good players is sound no matter where you play on the field, but it takes on increased importance when you are trying to finish a drive and score a touchdown.

The H receiver is one of the best athletes on the field for the Surface to Air System and he is the definition of a playmaker in space. This athlete gets many touches no matter where the ball is located but this area of the field starts to open some more special opportunities. If the play caller identifies that the defense wishes to play man coverage in this area of the field, then a Slant Wheel Concept to the H receiver can be a huge game changing play in this part of the field (Diagram 18-1).

The end zone is within easy reach from this part of the field and the Wheel Route can be a play that can, and in 2016 and 2017 has, scored many touchdowns. If the defense elects to switch to man coverage, as many do once, they lose ground on their side of the field, this play can easily end up with a linebacker or safety being asked to work to the flat and then run the length of the sideline with a very fast and nimble receiver like the H receiver in space.

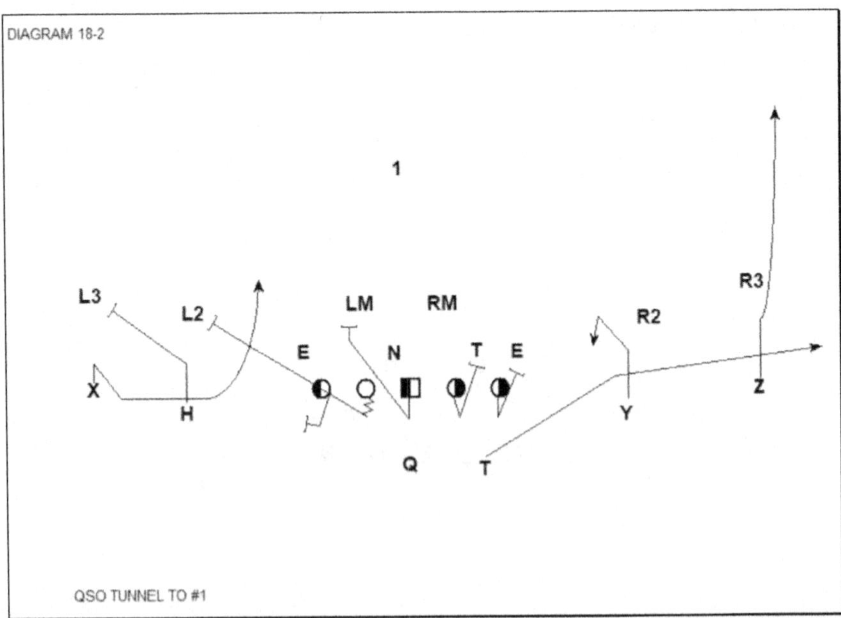

For years, slow screens have been a great way to attack defenses that bring pressure on this half of the field. The problem has been that play callers rarely know when the defense will bring pressure and thereby are guessing when the defense will elect to bring pressure and make themselves vulnerable to a slow screen. The Surface to Air System has created a package of plays that alleviates this worry and creates a safety value style of slow screens known as the QSO package.

QSO stands for Quick and Slow Option. Much like an RPO, this play features two different plays but this time it features some sort of quick pass play paired with a slow screen. The play caller can call any quick pass he wants and then pair it with a tunnel or slip screen. The first example of this that has been successful is the Snag Concept from a 2x2 alignment paired with a back-door Tunnel Screen to the outside receiver (Diagram 18-2).

This type of play is a huge advantage for the offense because of the defense plays zone then the Snag Concept is likely to win versus a variety of coverages and provide the offense with a great opportunity for a completion and a run after the catch. However, if the defense brings pressure than the quarterback can hold the football and throw the Tunnel Screen and likely bust the defense wide open for a big play. The offense can call these plays free from the constraint of really knowing what the defense is electing to pay from a coverage standpoint. That fact makes three great plays once the offense has passed the fifty-yard line. Another great variation of this package is to play from a 3x1 set and execute the same Snag Concept to the field with a Slip Screen concept by the tailback back to the boundary side of the field (Diagram 18-3).

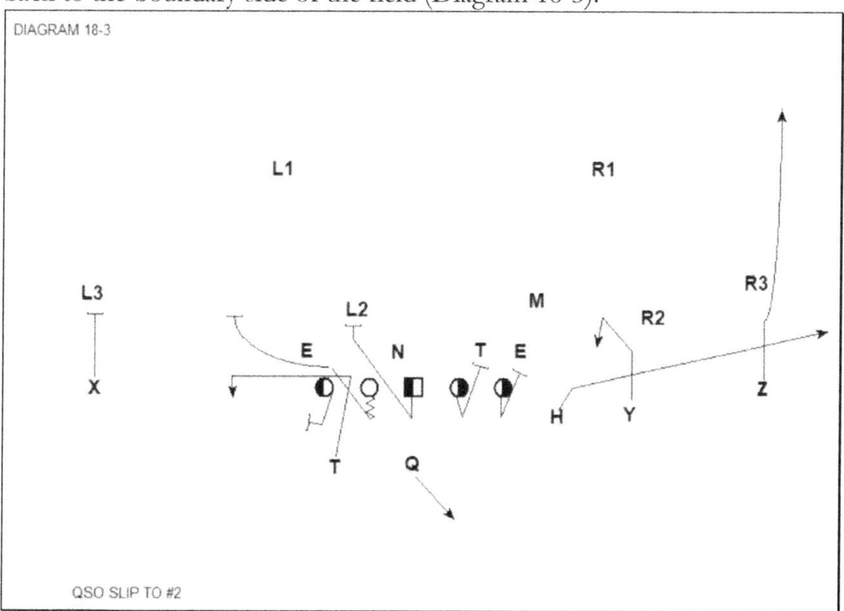

The offense can throw Tunnel Screens or Slip Screens out the back door of these QSO packages. The concept or front door side of the formation can feature essentially any play that the play caller wishes to utilize. These plays are extremely versatile, and they allow the play caller to attack the entire football field no matter what type of coverage the defense decides to play. This sort of flexibility allows the offense to be extremely lethal and flexible and place a great deal of pressure on the defense. These plays continue the mantra of players and not plays. The play caller can decide which athlete is his game breaker on the back door of the ball and assign him the slow screen while providing easy throws to the quarterback on the front door side should he need to pursue that avenue.

The offense will not abandon RPOs in this section of the field but the RPOs that are run in this part of the field are more structured to make sure that athletes can play in space. The quarterback is always a threat to run and can pull the ball at any point in the Surface to Air System but in this area of the field the offense is much more inclined to make sure the quarterback is a running threat because it makes the defense play eleven on eleven. One such RPO is to execute GY Counter from a stacked alignment and allow the quarterback the opportunity to pull the football and play in space (Diagram 18-4).

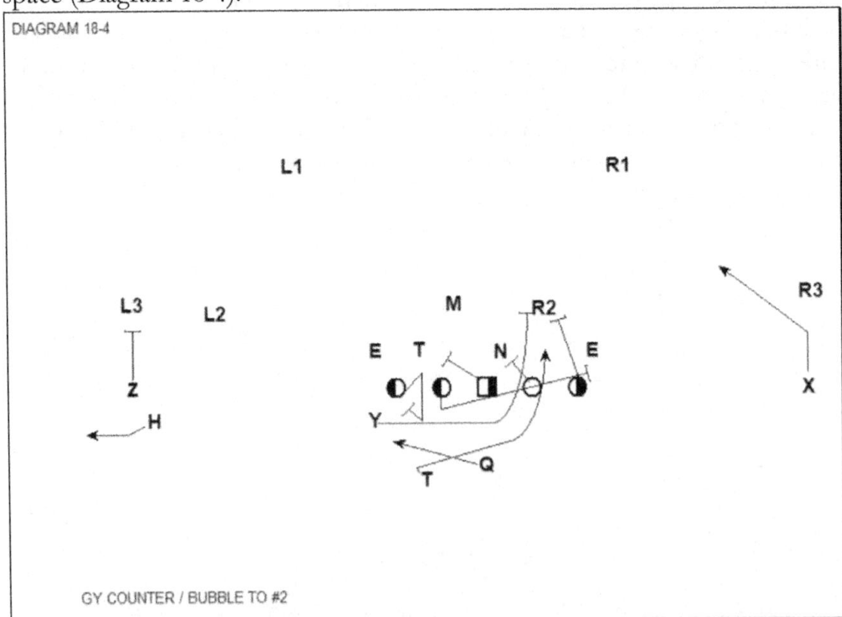

For many years, the Surface to Air System has augmented its touchdowns in this area of the field by allowing the quarterback to run the football more once it crosses the fifty-yard line. It is not simply a matter of running the quarterback but also structuring formations and plays that enhance the likelihood that the quarterback will end up with the ball in his hands.

This sort of formation isolates the defensive end and dares him to take away the tailback because if he doesn't the offense will have a play with many blockers at the point of attack. When the defensive end takes away the dive, he is leaving the entire edge of the defense vulnerable to attack and the L2 is trapped between the quarterback and the H receiver in a true post-snap triple option look. When the offense begins to play eleven on eleven in this part of the field there is a greater likelihood of big plays and a violation of the defense's basic structures. Defenses don't like the quarterback running the football on post-snap RPOs because it leaves their defense distorted and forces them to make tackles in space against superior skilled athletes. These are all the sorts of things that offense should be attempting to do in this portion of the field.

Plays That Alter the Launch Point

Another great idea in this portion of the field is to change the launch point of the quarterback. That is just a fancy term for rolling the quarterback out or bootlegging him out of the backfield. In this next section we will look at plays that attempt to remove the quarterback from his traditional location in the pocket. This is an advantage because it not only buys more time to complete the pass, but it also confuses pressure schemes and it provides the option for the quarterback to keep the ball and run should the pass play break down.

The first and perhaps easiest way for the offense to change the launch point is the more traditional sprint out. One of the better concepts we have run the last few years from a sprint-outlook is the Spot Pivot Concept from a 2x2 set (Diagram 18-5).

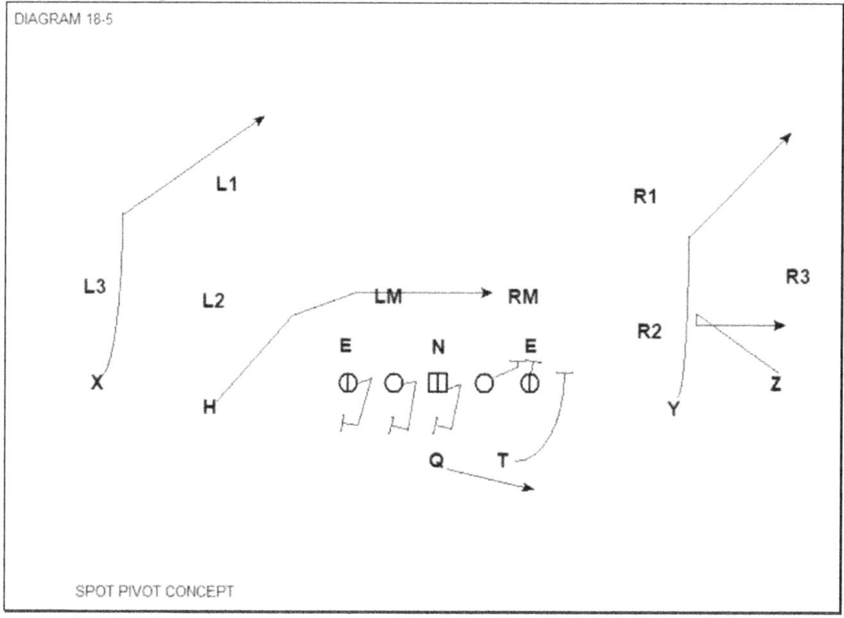

The back-door Post Route and Under Route are great man coverage beating concepts that work into the quarterback's line of site. The Corner

Route and the Pivot Route are also great routes to attack man coverage. In addition, if the defense takes all these routes and outnumbers the defense, then the quarterback can continue rolling and outflank the defense by running the football. If the defense was in some sort of zone coverage and bailed multiple defenders into the route structure, then the quarterback would be able to easily scramble for a short gain and keep the drive's momentum going. Finally, his sort of launch point variation destroys the defense's confidence in bring significant amounts of middle pressure for fear of being outflanked by the offense with the quarterback leaving the backfield.

Another great way to change the launch point is using bootleg passes. There are two main types of bootleg passes that we feature in the Surface to Air System and both are designed to sell the defense that they are watching an RPO and then be struck with a deep pass. The first bootleg pass is a play that simulates a split inside zone call with a Naked Bootleg Play and then attacks the back half of the defensive secondary (Diagram 18-6).

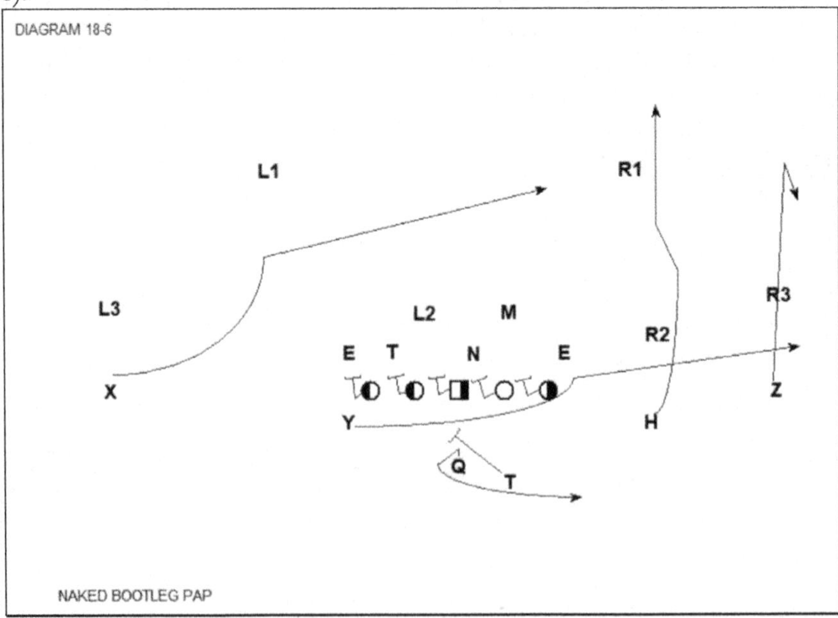

This play will have a deep Comeback Route on the outside with a Seam Route running the safety off. The backside X receiver runs the deep Over Route while the sniffer fakes the split zone and then continues to the flat. The quarterback can sell the RPO and the escape as the sniffer hits and slows the defensive end and keeps him from containing the edge of the defense. The split zone action in the backfield dramatically slows the defense and forces them to play honest on the RPO style of the play and leaves them vulnerable to the deep breaking routes built into the play.

The second type of bootleg play is G Scheme Bootleg Play that blocks the defensive end with a pulling guard after the backfield action sells outside zone (Diagram 18-7).

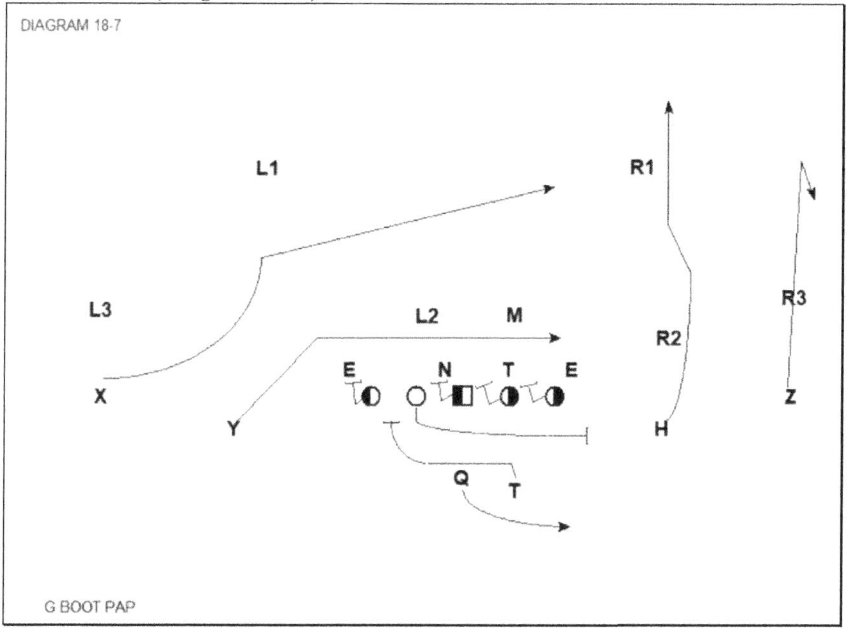

This play features a Shake Corner Route and a Skinny Post route on the front side of the route combination with a deep Over Route and shallower Under Route crossing into the quarterback's line of sight. This change of launch point play is less deceptive than the Naked Bootleg Play but offers a higher degree of "Big on Big" protection for the quarterback.

These three plays combined offer a great way to attack the defenses vertically down the field after selling some sort of contradictory action at the outset of the play. These two bootleg plays leave the defense conflicted between the RPO and PAP (Play Action Pass) part of the Surface to Air System. This contradiction allows the offense to play more vertically down the field and take shots at scores while keeping the quarterback well protected and changing the launch point to allow him to use his mobility regardless of the defensive coverage.

Conclusion

When the offense crosses the fifty-yard line there must be a fundamental shift in the purpose of the play calling. The offense must, with each yard gained, assume that the odds of punting are less and less likely. Most high school punters cannot pin an opposing offense deep and so the net gain of a punt from the opponents forty-yard line are almost negligible.

Therefore, the offense is moving more and more into four down territory as it passes the fifty-yard line and progresses into the defense's territory. As a result, they style of plays that the play caller utilizes must begin to take on a more aggressive posture.

The play caller must be prepared for the defense to pay to the extremes of either dropping or blitzing multiple defenders. The answer in this portion of the field must be varied as we have mentioned above. The focus should be on finding ways to get the ball to your best players and letting the operate in green grass and make plays to put touchdowns on the board. The game of football is won with touchdowns and not with field goals. Therefore, a play caller needs to be aggressive in this area and get the ball to his best players in a variety of unique and explosive ways.

19
RED ZONE

Most people declare that the Red Zone starts at the twenty-yard line but that is simply not our belief. The twenty-yard line is just a landmark that is part of the larger free-wheeling zone that extends from the fifty-yard line to the ten-yard line. The Surface to Air System Red Zone is designed to start at the ten-yard line and then extends to the end zone.

The goal of the system at this point is to score touchdowns. It is not acceptable to kick field goals. It is my belief that kicking field goals is a great way to lose high school football games. In 2015, we kicked many field goals and had a moderately successful season. We made the decision going into the 2016 season that we would practice the Red Zone more often.

We also made the decision that we would not alter our play calling until we made it to the ten-yard line instead of the twenty-yard line. Our final consideration was that we would alter the style of plays that we utilized in this area of the field. In 2015, we used to bring in heavy sets and just try to smash the football down people's' throats in a test of wills that often resulted in three instead of six points forced by the offense.

Starting in 2016, we utilized more one-word Red Zone calls that were built, practiced, and specialized just for the ten-yard line and in. These plays were run almost every day and they were tailored to attack specific aspects of the defense that we saw each week. These plays were built after lengthy study sessions of the defense and a careful analysis of what the defense was good at and what they were vulnerable to in these ten yards. Starting with the fall we began to practice plays from each of the last ten yards going into the Red Zone and we practice them almost every day. The results were that we broke the school passing record for touchdowns, the school record for PATs, and led the state in touchdowns scored this season.

The simple answer to success in the Red Zone is a steady dose of film analysis followed by a meticulous use of specialized plays designed to defeat each week's opponents Red Zone defense. The plays that follow in this chapter are just a sampling of the kinds of plays that made us such a successful Red Zone offense over the past two seasons.

Red Zone Plays

Over the past two seasons we have seen an increase in our touchdowns in the Red Zone, which we still track from the twenty-yard line for the sake of continuity with the general football community statistically, at over 80%. The reason for this change is partially that we began to practice Red Zone offense almost every day but there is a second reasons also. The second reason that our Red Zone efficiency went up is that we became much more aggressive. Our mentality is that we treat each snap inside the ten-yard line like it is a 4th Down call.

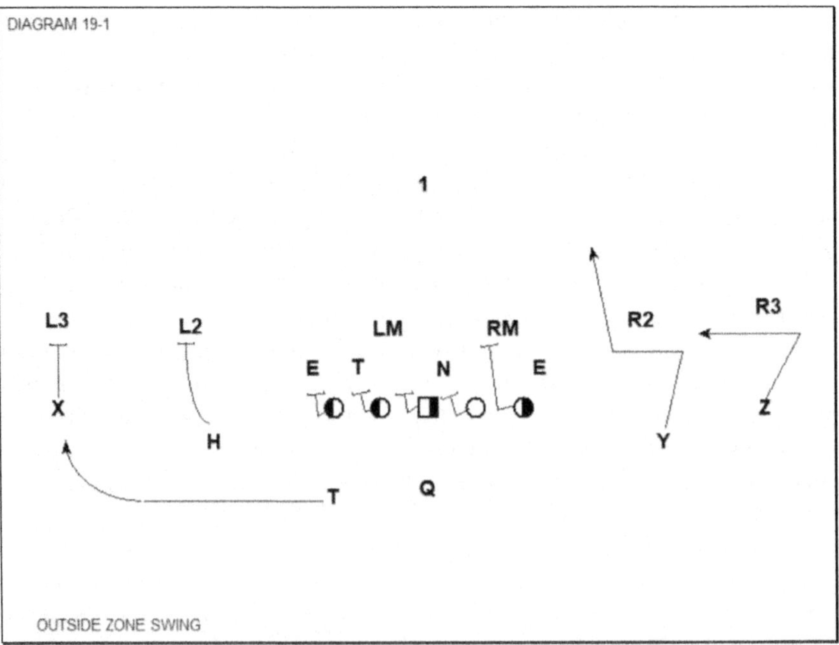

We basically trick ourselves into believing that each snap from 1st Down to 4th Down in this territory is a live or die down. We want the offense to feel the game changes on every snap here and every snap must result in a touchdown. This increased aggressive tendency has led to more touchdowns. We will start at the more simplistic ways we have tried to score touchdowns and work to the more "window dressed" versions throughout this chapter.

The first play we feature in this area is the outside zone executed from the Swing Screen by the tailback (Diagram 19-1).

Here our goal is to get the ball outside quickly because we will assume on this play, and all plays in this section for the sake of simplicity, that the defense is going to load the box and play man coverage. The tailback is an extra hat on the perimeter that a linebacker must defend very quickly by the quarterback can run the ball or throw the back-door Grass Concept if he feels that the Swing Route has been sniffed out. Our goal here is to expand the defense make a defensive player that is there to be a run stopper, a linebacker, and make him a chaser in space.

A second and much more complicated way to score touchdowns is through a one-word concept we have given many names, but we utilize for its ability to create six options to score the football (Diagram 19-2).

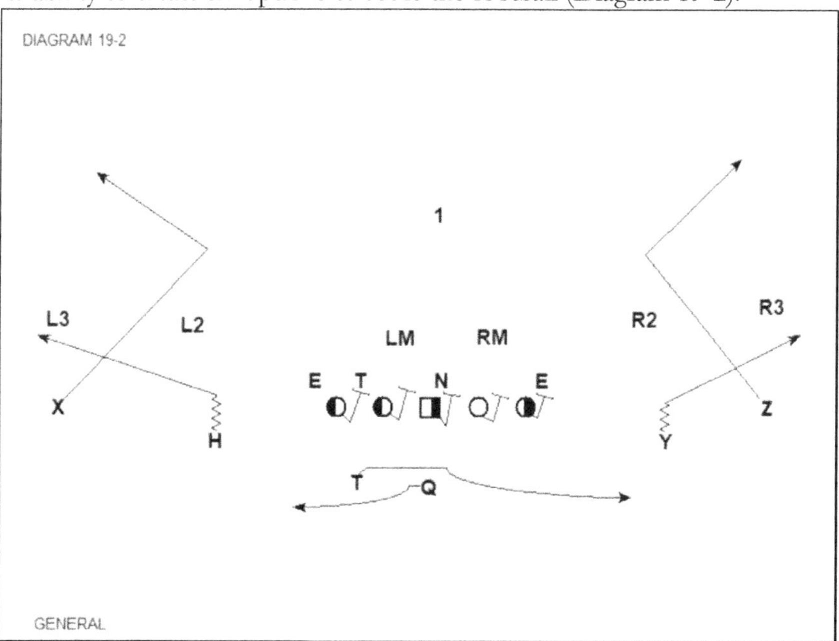

This play has the offensive lineman running outside zone to the right, but they are holding up their blocks and staying at the line of scrimmage after executing reach blocks. The quarterback reads the back side defensive end and if he chases the quarterback will pull the ball and have three options including the V Cut Corner Route, Stutter Flat Route, or running the ball in the end zone himself. If the defensive end feathers, then the ball is handed to the tailback and he has the same three options on his side of the formation. This play gives the offense six options to score the football that are balanced on both sides of the formation. This play is a staple for us inside the five-yard line and or trying to convert on two-point conversions. This is not a play that can just be thrown into the game plan. This play requires a great deal of attention and it requires practice and we devote that time because coming away with six instead of three points is a core portion of our offensive philosophy.

Another one word call we utilize focus on a 3x1 stack set with man coverage beating routes from a roll out posture (Diagram 19-3).

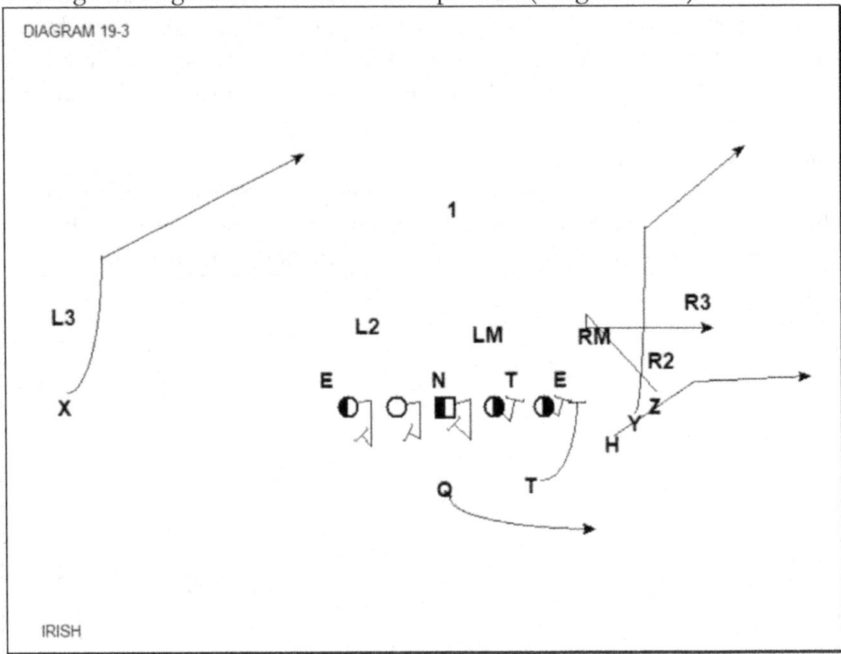

The middle receiver executes a Corner Route to the back pylon, the third receiver runs a Flat Route at the front pylon, and the first receiver pushes inside to take a defender with him and then pivots back to the flat to give the quarterback a great outlet to throw the ball. The backside receiver runs between the uprights and gives the quarterback a throwback option there as well. The quarterback has four pass options and can also elect to run the football. This one-word play is a great option when the offense first makes it to the ten-yard line and so there is more room to operate. Once again, this play is repeatedly run throughout the week, so the offensive personnel can get used to their landmarks and the quarterback can see the routes and where they are likely to break open.

The Surface to Air System has not abandoned the idea of executing RPOs in this part of field, quite the contrary, the offense is full of these types of plays for this area. The RPOs that we use here are designed to get the offense on an eleven on eleven posture with the defense by running the quarterback. However, the offense does not wish to line up in 3x2 because it might not allow us the same ability to confuse the defense when they are in man coverage. So, we want to get five receivers out and run the quarterback, but we don't wish to let the defense see we are in empty. A great way to do this is to run the GY Counter but to read the defensive end with a Swing Read (Diagram 19-4).

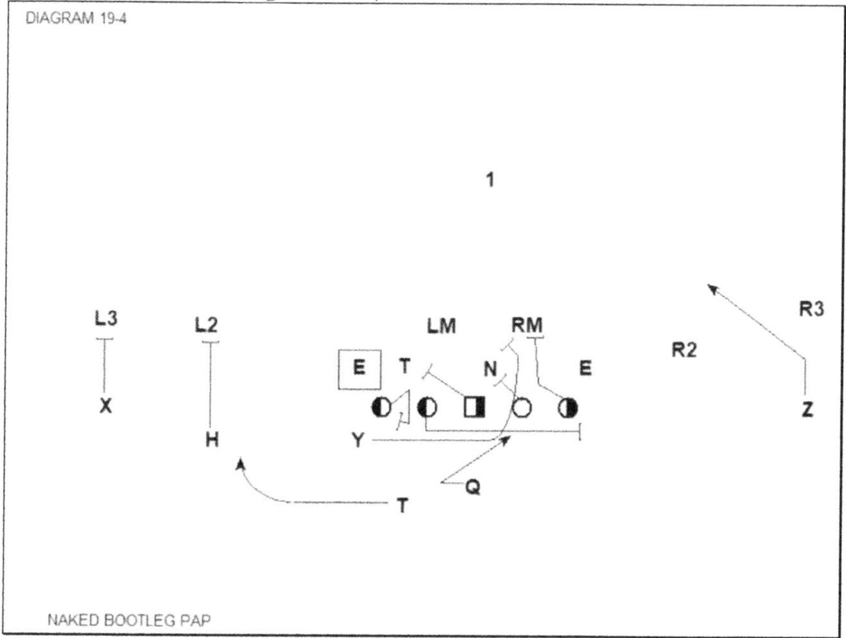

The quarterback reads the defensive end and if he feathers with the Swing Route then the quarterback runs the football but if the defensive end plays the quarterback then the ball will be thrown to the tailback. If the ball is thrown to the tailback then the linebacker covering him is conflicted and likely caught in traffic attempting to leave the box. If the defensive end takes the tailback then the offense has a hat for a hat and the quarterback is the extra man in the box running the football. This style of RPO is basically an empty RPO but we are not allowing the defense to see that it is a quarterback run with five receivers out in the progression until it is too late for them to adjust their defense.

Another great version of this style of RPO is the sniffer tight end insertion paired with a Flat Route Screen by the tailback (Diagram 19-5).

The offensive lineman will run a locked inside zone to the right with the sniffer bending back into the back-door B gap to block the first linebacker in that gap. The tailback comes off the hip of the sniffer to run the Flat Route and thereby force the linebacker on the right side of the formation to determine if he will remain in the box or take the back in man coverage.

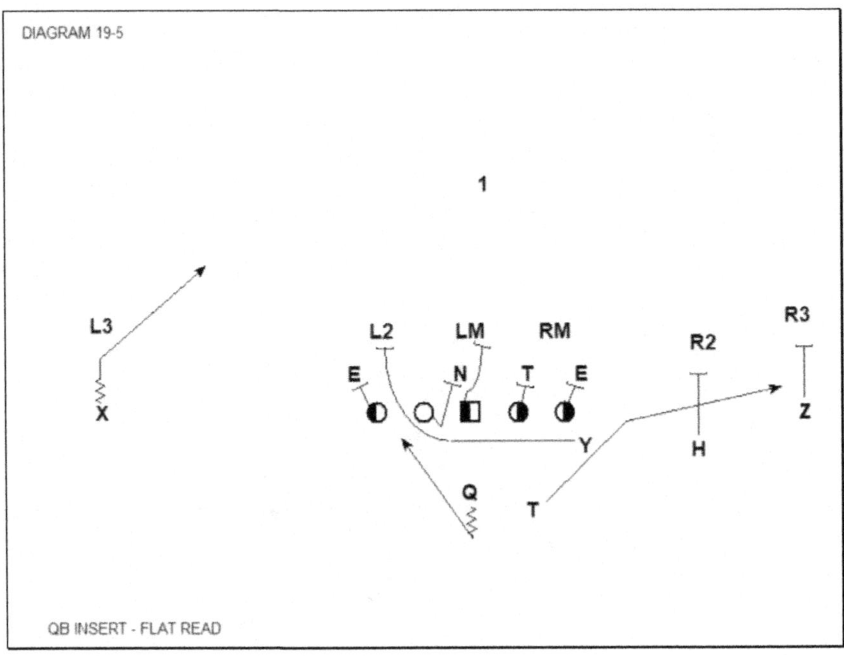

If the linebacker leaves the box with the tailback then the quarterback runs what is essentially an Isolation Play. If, however, the linebacker does not leave the box then the quarterback will throw the Flat Route to the tailback that will outflank the defense. These types of RPOs feature use of all five of the skilled athletes on the field and the running ability of the quarterback. The other thing this play does is it allows all six athletes to be involved in the play without showing the defense pre-snap that it will be an empty RPO.

Conclusion

The Red Zone, for us in the Surface to Air System, starts at the ten-yard line and proceeds to the goal line. We still track our Red Zone efficiency using the twenty-yard line to keep us with the standard norms in the game of football. However, we do not change our play calling until we reach the ten-yard line.

Over the past two season we have scored a touchdown over 80% of the time when we cross the twenty-yard line. This success is a manifestation of hard work, players who buy into our system, and a heavy emphasis in practice of Red Zone repetitions. We are successful in the Red Zone because we spend a great deal of time on it. The age-old adage of what you spend your time on will become your treasure is true for us in this instance. We want to win in the Red Zone and finish off drives and therefore we watch an inordinate amount of film on this area of the field and we practice it every day. We also build plays, like those we discussed above, that are specifically designed to win in these tight quarters and use the defense's goal line defense against it.

20
THE ART VS THE SCIENCE OF PLAY CALLING

In the Surface to Air System we feel that play-calling is basically a manifestation of both the art and the science of play-calling. We feel that there must be a steady and consistent dose of Science in the sense that the play-caller must watch film, must analyze his opponent's, and must self-scout himself in order to come up with the best solution possible. So, the game is a science experiment where the play caller analyzes data and synthesizes what he sees and tests it throws out the week to come up with the best solution to a pre-ordained problem. The play caller must use the empirical method when he builds his game plan and he must understand the structure of his own offense as well as that the of the defense. He must use a whole host of data, physics, and metrics to call plays effectively.

A play caller also must operate without the benefit of science. He must paint with a fine brush and call plays based upon such non-scientific prospects that are used every game like his gut, his instincts, or the feel he has at that moment in the game. The play caller must truly feel his way through the game more than he can think about odds and about reason. He must analyze less and feel the tenor and tone of the game more. He must sense what the defense is attempting to do, and he must feel what the offense is capable of in a moment.

Then begs the question is all play-calling essentially a manifestation of both the science and the art of these two competing ideas? Personally, I have always felt that game planning is a large amount of science and the play calling is a large amount of art. However, it is probably more practical that both are in play in the game plan and both are in play during the play calling aspects of preparation and implementation of the game. A coach must be able to process out the game from a scientific standpoint, but he also must be able to feel his way through and understand how his players and his opponent are operating throughout the game.

I feel that there are coaches that can get by and be successful being purveyors of science and others can be successful leaning on the art of play calling. As I progress into my twentieth year of coaching, and the last majority calling plays, I come to realize that the science and the art of play calling are intertwined. I lean more heavily on science in game planning and more in the art of play calling.

However, I use both interchangeably and across the spectrum without even realizing it sometimes. I feel that more emphasis will be placed on science behind play calling because it is a growing trend in our sport. More coaches will be trained to call plays by watching film, analyzing the data, and studying the analytics behind the game. These trends are positive, and they should and must continue to grow in our game. It should be pointed out, however, that the art of play calling must not go away. A coach must still be able to use his intuition to decide where the contest is going and what is the best decision. I have many times stood on a sideline in the fall and call a play that helps win the game despite that fact that there's no scientific reason for me to call it. The reason I called it is because I felt that the players on the field needed me to make that call at that moment for our team to be successful. Therefore, as science continues to march on and continues to ingrain itself into our game, we should accept and embrace it. We should use data, analytics, and we should study tendencies and trends. We should use science in and technology in the weight room and on the football field.

While we are doing this, we should also remember that the human element is the core of our profession. What we as humans feel, think, and perceive is at the heart of what makes us good play callers. We must know ourselves and we must know our opponents. We must feel the game and its progress. We must feel if the moment is right for us to strike or the moment pleads for caution. The Surface to Air System is a cross section or better stated it is a meeting point of the science and the art of play calling. We will utilize the science behind the game while continuing to practice your art. In short, we will be like Einstein proposing and testing theories while at the same time keeping our easel and brushes close at hand just like Rembrandt.

21
CONCLUSION

I started calling plays for the first time in the Fall of 1999. I have been calling plays across these twenty years with varied results. When I started out calling plays I did so by purchasing a book and scribbling down all the plays that I could understand and giving those plays funny names and hoping for the best. Twenty years later our teams led the state in almost every offensive category and broke most of the school records along the way. Now we have young men leaving their names in the school and state record books. So, the question must be begged what happened?

Well, first I got older and more experienced. That is without a doubt the biggest and most obvious solution to the problem of how to get better at play calling, is to simply get more experience doing it. The more often you do something the better you get at it. I also started to attend more clinics. I attended my local state clinics, Nike Clinics, Glazier Clinics, and almost any other football gathering that I could afford to attend. I also started to call college and high school coaches that I thought did a great job and started to hang out with them and ask them questions. I asked them about how they did things.

These sorts of formal and informal meetings certainly helped but they were lacking in a major area. The coaches that I went to hang out with might share a play or two, and there were many who would share almost nothing, but they rarely if ever gave away any "secret sauce" like how do they game plan or call their plays. These coaches either did not wish to charge what they knew, or they did not feel that communicating these items was valuable. There were a select few that did share not only their playbooks but also their insights into how to structure a game.

After a while I started to realize that each of these coaches really didn't have a secret as much as they each had their own way of doing things. I realized that building game plans and calling plays would be a great extent about who I was rather than what I knew. I had to first define who I was as a builder and caller. I had to find out what sort of offense I wanted to run and what sort of style I wanted to play. In short, I had to define who I was as a coach. Once I had defined who I was, then I had to refine it. I used to be a grinder watching the film repeatedly for long hours to game plan.

I have now refined that strategy and I watch film much less, but I look for specific things like the matchup, the leverage, and the grass. I used to not worry about Red Zone and assumed I would just score when I got there and now, I am almost pathological about preparing for that area of the field. I used to not have a philosophy about what to do on a certain down or distance and now I have just completed my second book discussing it in quite extensive detail.

I feel there needs to be a constant revision and redefining of who and what you are as a game planner and play caller on an almost year by year basis. If there is not a constant evolution in this area, then you will become stagnant. That is another great point, grow. There needs to be a commitment and a passion to constantly evolve and grow inside the game.

I once read about Nick Saban and how he was not a fan of tempo, spread offenses, or RPOs and now when you watch Alabama play you essentially see all of these as part of their repertoire. The reason for this is that Coach Saban wants to win worse than he wants to stay stagnant and safe. He must learn and grow outside his comfort zone to get better. There are things he will never change and there are things he will change. The quality game planner and play caller must decipher what must be changed and when and what must not be compromised on for it is a part of the winning formula every year.

Another major component of my growth as a coach in the area of game planning and play calling has been the creation, expansion, and evolution of my consulting business, the Surface to Air System. Since Summer 2017 we have had over 100 coaches join our consulting group. These coaches need help, advice, council, and support in different areas of the game of football. Some of these coaches text questions, some tweet, some call, and some require me to come to their campus and install the offense in person.

All these coaches are on the cutting edge of our craft because they reach out to a fraternity like ours to get better and ask more questions. These coaches look over the horizon and they ask about the unknown. These coaches wish to know more about game planning and they wish to know more about play calling. Their thirst for more has led them to inquire about it inside our group. Their thirst for this knowledge has compelled me to better define my own views in these areas so that I can better explain my philosophy to these coaches. As a consultant I can no longer just share a play with a coach and say that it works. I must be able to explain how they play fits into a game plan and then how and in what situation it should be called on game night.

The fraternity of coaches in the Surface to Air System have a genuine and growing thirst for knowledge in the area of game planning and play calling. These coaches wish to know more about how to construct plays and how to call them in a game setting. I have written this book because I feel it covers new ground in the area of game planning and play calling. I do not feel this book answers every question, but it does provide a strong framework for the planner/caller in preparing a modern RPO based offense.

For me, this book has helped me to grow because it has forced me to reach into my own mind and see how I have been successful and articulate the actual process behind that success. I have had to identify my own thirst for knowledge and then I have had to look over the horizon to find the answer. This book is not a full story of all the answers over that horizon because neither I nor any other coach on earth has all the answers. But this book is a peek over the horizon and a small revelation of why a game plan and a play call system that I have made work is useful to the reader. I hope that this work has served some use to you and that it helps you to define or refine your own approach to the game of football in the area of game planning and play calling.

I hope this work has pushed your understanding and your imagination forward. I hope that this book has made you love or fall in love again with the beautiful art and science of game planning and calling plays and I hope it helps you get more 1st Downs and score more touchdowns. I also hope this book in some small way helps make the game of football better. And Finally, I hope this book makes you in some small way a better coach who does a better job taking care of kids and making them appreciate and love this great game that has done so much for all of us.

Thanks for reading and God Bless each of you!

ABOUT THE AUTHOR

Rich Hargitt has been a football coach since 1999. He has served as a head football coach and offensive coordinator at the high school level in Illinois, Indiana, North Carolina, and South Carolina. In 2010, he earned a Master of Arts Degree in Physical Education with Coaching Specialization from Ball State University. Hargitt's teams have utilized the Air Raid Offense to upset several quality teams and the offense has produced school record holders in rushing and passing. Coach Hargitt's first Air Raid Quarterback, Mitch Niekamp, holds several college records at Illinois College and is currently a starting Quarterback in Europe's professional leagues. He previously contributed to a six-part video series on the Spread Wing-T offense for *American Football Monthly* and has been published numerous times in coaching journals on the Air Raid Offense. He has spoken for both the Nike Coach of the Clinics and the Glazier Clinics about the Air Raid Offense. His first book *101 Shotgun Wing-T Plays* was published by Coaches Choice in 2012. Coach Hargitt's second book *101 Air Raid Plays* was published by Coaches Choice in 2013. Hargitt's third book, *Coaching the Air Raid Offense,* was published in 2014. Hargitt's fourth and fifth books, *Packaging Plays in the Air Raid Offense and Play Calling for the Air Raid Offense*, were released in January of 2015. The 6th book in the Hargitt collection, *Coaching the RPO Offense,* was released in 2016. The 7th work by Hargitt, *101 RPO Plays, was* released in 2017. Coach Hargitt's 8th work was titled *Teaching and Installing the RPO* which was released in 2017 and his 9th work was titled *Surface to Air System Summer Manual; 2018 Edition* and was released in 2018. Coach Hargitt has also collaborated with Coaches Choice on a series of DVDs detailing the Air Raid Offense. Hargitt brought the Air Raid Offense to Nation Ford High School in 2011 where he helped lead the Falcons to their first non-losing season, first AAA Region victory, first AAA Playoff berth, and first AAA Playoff victory. In 2012, Hargitt's offense broke the school single game and single season offensive records for passing yards, touchdowns, and points scored. Also, in 2012, Hargitt helped lead Nation Ford HS to the AAAA playoffs for the first time in school history. In 2013, Hargitt helped lead the Ashbrook Greenwave to the second round of NCHSAA AAA playoffs and a 9-4 overall record. He is currently the Assistant Head Coach/Offensive Coordinator at Eastside HS in Taylors, SC. In 2015 Hargitt's offense achieved a statewide Top 10 ranking, averaged 383 yards per game (231 passing, 152 rushing), finished ranked in the Top 10 of the state and Top 5 of AAA in passing, achieved 2nd non-losing season in 13 years. In 2016 the offense improved even further as the team advanced to the SCHSL AAAA Playoffs. In addition, the offense averaged 488 yards per game (286 passing, 202 rushing) and 41 points per game in the regular season and finished the season in AAAA ranked 4th in rushing (2,127 yards), 3rd in rushing touchdowns (27), 1st in passing (3,311 yards), 1st in yards passing per game (301), 1st in pass completions (257), 1st in pass attempts (365), 1st in passing touchdowns (37), 1st in completion percentage (70%), 1st in touchdowns scored (65), 1st in scoring (453), 1st in PATs made (53) and 1st in total yardage from scrimmage (5,438 yards). The offense also led the State of South Carolina in Total Yardage from Scrimmage (5,438 yards). The 2016 offense also featured a quarterback that completed the 3rd most passes in a game and 3rd most touchdown passes in a single game in state history. In addition, the offense featured a receiver that the 4th most passes in a single game and 6th most passes in a season in state history. Hargitt's 2017 Southside HS team broke the school single game passing record and the school single season passing record. In addition, the offense finished the regular season ranked in AAA 6th in rushing (1082 yards), 1st in passing yards (2328 yards), 1st in completions (192), 1st in pass attempts (318), 1st in passing touchdowns (21), and 3rd in completion percentage (60%). Hargitt led the tigers to a 7 point per game improvement from the year before he arrived and helped lead the Tigers to the SCHSL AAA playoffs. Coach Hargitt accepted the Head Football position at Emmett High School in Emmett, Idaho in the Spring of 2018. Hargitt's Emmett HS team finished 1st in the Idaho AAAA classification in pass attempts (242), pass completions (394), and passing yards (2,656 yards). Hargitt resides in Middleton, Idaho with his wife Lisa and their sons Griffin and Graham.

Made in the USA
Middletown, DE
28 November 2018